This is the Church of St. Stephen
Anoka, Minnesota

The Church of St. Stephen is one of the largest parishes in the Archdiocese of St. Paul and Minneapolis with 4100 households. In response to the Community's vitality and on-going growth, a building expansion project was completed in 1999 that added a daily Mass chapel, adoration chapel, community center, nursery, and office complex. The parish also sponsors a K-8 grade school with an enrollment of 460.

The parish is served by three priests from the Crosier Community of Anoka. Decision making is broad based and collegial. The Pastor works very closely with the Pastoral and Finance Councils. In addition, there are five advisory Commissions of eight to twelve members each in the areas of worship, formation, pastoral care, resource development-communication, and school.

The parish's mission is to be a community of faith that fosters the formation of Catholics who practice Gospel values in their daily lives. St. Stephen's wants to distinguish itself for the hospitality that the members offer to each other and to guests, the quality of its liturgies, support to families, and outreach to those in the area.

" You shall be my people "

Ezekiel 37

A history of the
Archdiocese of
Saint Paul and
Minneapolis

By

Sister John Christine Wolkerstorfer, C.S.J., Ph. D.

Author : Sister John Christine Wolkerstorfer, C. S. J., Ph. D
Cover photos : Basilica of Saint Mary, Minneapolis
            Cathedral of Saint Paul, Saint Paul
            Father Hennepin, an early missionary to the territory, christens the Falls of St. Anthony
Cover design by Barb Lappi
Cover photos by Doug Ohman, Pioneer Photography, New Hope, MN
Publisher : Editions du Signe - B.P. 94 - 67038 Strasbourg - France
Design and Layout : Juliette Roussel
Director of Publication : Dr. Claude-Bernard Costecalde
Copyright Text : © The Archdiocese of Saint Paul and Minneapolis 1999
Copyright Design and Layout : © 1999 Editions du Signe - ISBN 2-87718-898-1
Printed in France by PPO Graphic, 93500 Pantin

*F*oreword

Dear friends in Christ,

We are indeed privileged to be living during such a great confluence of historical milestones - the 150th Anniversary of the founding of the Archdiocese of Saint Paul and Minneapolis and the 2000th anniversary of the birth of our Lord Jesus Christ.

Through the hard work and pioneering spirit of the people who founded this diocese in a tiny log cabin church on the banks of the Mississippi River, a path of success was created which we have been following and benefiting from ever since. In one way, the work of those early missionary priests, sisters, brothers and lay people seems a world apart from our modern Church experience at the very end of the 20th century. Yet the message they shared with the natives as well as immigrants who teemed into this prosperous land is the same today as it was then - Christ has died, Christ has risen and Christ will come again.

My hope is that this book commemorating the years of change, struggle and triumph for the people of the Archdiocese of Saint Paul and Minneapolis will find a prominent place in our homes, our parishes and our schools. It is a rich resource for remembering our past as well as a guide for growth in the future.

As Archbishop, I am privileged to serve the people of this Archdiocese and to celebrate this most joyous occasion with you. Please join with me as we make this 150th Anniversary one that truly brings greater glory and honor to our Lord Jesus Christ.

Sincerely yours in Christ,

† Harry J. Flynn

Most Reverend Harry J. Flynn, D.D.
Archbishop of Saint Paul and Minneapolis

Shepherds of the Archdiocese of Saint Paul and Minneapolis

Preface

The year 2000 marks a special time of rejoicing for the people of God in the Archdiocese of St. Paul and Minneapolis. They can look with pride to 150 years of saying "yes" to the call of Christ to live and spread His message of love to the world. Thankful for God's grace which has made their achievements possible, they now face the challenge of a new age with the hope and promise that God will continue to be with them. They must be ever ready as God's chosen people to further the work of the Church in serving all people, showing them how to live that Gospel message. As American Catholics attempt to make the Gospel message relevant to the changing times, they will build on all that the Church in America has accomplished before them. So it shall be for Catholics in the Archdiocese of Saint Paul and Minneapolis as they contribute to the vitality of their local Church as future challenges arise.

Minnesota's development into statehood emerged amid the migration of various ethnic groups who chose to make their homes near the headwaters of the Mississippi River. Here an indigenous culture had predated the immigrants' arrival. The dedicated missionaries, Catholic priests, and religious men and women who came to serve the Native Americans and immigrants are important to the story. The Catholic Church that evolved in 19th-century America was indeed an immigrant Church, conditioned strongly by Church practices established in Europe. Much was accomplished under this model of Church, and an increasing call from the laity to live the Gospel message brought forth a keener understanding that the laity's role was essential in bringing that message to everyday life. The bishops, clergy, religious, and laity were all mandated to strive personally and collaboratively to further the work of Christ's Church. Christ's emphasis on the dignity of every person permeated the evolution of understanding Church as a pluralistic image, where all were welcome. The American democratic experience conditioned the Church in America for this change.

The Archdiocese, through the Communications Office, has made this project possible. Special thanks are due the personnel at the Archdiocesan Archives and *The Catholic Spirit (Catholic Bulletin)*, Archbishop Harry Flynn, and others for materials and insights shared. My own religious community, the Sisters of St. Joseph of Carondelet, has made it possible for me to become well acquainted with the history of the Archdiocese through my work as a teacher and historian. For this I am grateful. It is the hope of the author that all who read this book will share the pride in what good has been accomplished for the greater Church in this local Church of the Archdiocese of St. Paul and Minneapolis. While striving to preserve integrity of meaning, the author has used inclusive language in the quotations from the Vatican II Documents.

More than any other event in modern times the Second Vatican Council focused on and universally changed the understanding of Church from an authoritarian model to one of people serving people as Christ did. This pluralistic model fit more closely with what Catholics were experiencing in the Archdiocese of St. Paul and Minneapolis during the 1960s.

This brief history shows the influence of the immigrant Church of the Archdiocese of St. Paul and Minneapolis as it evolved during the 19th century into a dynamic pluralistic People of God in the 20th century. The development of today's local Church in this region reflects all the human successes and failures of the constantly changing historic scene. Nevertheless, being solidly grounded in the Gospel of Jesus Christ and trusting in Divine assistance, that Church moves steadily toward fulfillment of God's will for His people. Faith, hope, and charity carry us into the next millennium.

Sister John Christine Wolkerstorfer, C.S.J., Ph. D.

6

Jaques Frances Lee, "Rock at Crooked Lake", oil on convas, 1947 (Minnesota Historical Society)

"*Nor is God remote from those who in shadows and images seek the unknown God, since He gives to all persons life and breath and all things, and since the Savior wills all to be saved.*"

Lumen Gentium

Indian woman and child in elk tooth dresses, 1880 (Minnesota Historical Society)

The presence of the Catholic Church in the development of American history attests to the influence of the Spirit in calling all people to union with their God by living out Christ's Gospel message in each age. From the founding of our country through the opening of lands in the Midwest to the waves of immigrant settlers, the Catholic Church has been an integral part of the development of the Midwest. Even before the early missionaries made their way into the wooded plains and grasslands of the upper Mississippi River region, Indian tribes there, especially the Sioux and Chippewa, sought a union with a Higher Being through various forms of nature and creation but with no knowledge of Christ's gospel message. The pantheism and native culture of Minnesota's indigenous tribes created a milieu in America's heartland that lured many missionary zealots to the region in answer to Christ's call to "go and teach all nations." Early Jesuit and Recollect Fathers came with the intent of saving souls for Christ and doing away with all that spoke of "paganism" to the people of their time. Throughout the growth of the Archdiocese of St. Paul-Minneapolis, the Catholic Church has endeavored to meet the spiritual and corporal needs of the diverse groups that comprise the community called to live out the gospel message as Catholics.

Chapel and buildings at Pembina, 1840

7

Dakota duck hunter on the upper Mississippi, 1858 (Minnesota Historical Society)

St. Paul's Chapel, Saint Paul 1841

When the nations of Europe were in fierce competition to control the North American continent, explorers, voyageurs, and missionaries traversed the region, leaving their mark in fur-trading posts, forts, and chapels. In 1680 Sieur Du Luth reached the fringes of what is now Ramsey County in Minnesota as he paddled down the St. Croix and Mississippi Rivers and area waterways. In that same year Father Louis Hennepin was in the area of Phalen Creek, discovered and named St. Anthony Falls, and was captured by a party of Dakota Indians in southern Minnesota. Jesuits set up the Chapel of St. Michael the Archangel at Fort Beauharnois near Frontenac as early as 1727. Father Charles Mesaiger set out with 50 soldiers and voyageurs from Montreal and erected Fort St. Charles in the Northwest Angle inlet of Lake of the Woods. Here he also set up a chapel. It was here that the French Recollect priest, Father Aulneau, and his expedition from Montreal were massacred by hostile Indians in 1735. The northeastern part of the area that would become Minnesota

1. Reverend Lucien Galtier

2. Reverend Pierz, Indian Missionary

3. Bishop Loras of Dubuque who sent early missionaries into the Minnesota Territory

saw much missionary work by the Rev. Francis Xavier Pierz, a Slovenian priest from Michigan. He was instrumental in founding the Grand Portage Mission near the mouth of the Pigeon River where he and the Chippewa built a chapel dedicated to St. Peter. Lord Selkirk's colony had a chapel dedicated to St. Francis Xavier which served the Chippewa, French, and "half-breeds" in the Pembina region as early as 1818. Many of the Selkirk settlers found their way south to the Fort Snelling Reserve, at the confluence of the Mississippi and Minnesota rivers. It was in this region, just west of the fort that the river landing, eventually called St. Paul, would grow. In 1841 the river port was named after the chapel erected on the bluff above the landing and dedicated to St. Paul the apostle. This first log chapel "cathedral" had been built by Father Lucien Galtier, a missionary sent by Bishop Loras of the Dubuque Diocese in Iowa.

By 1845 some 30 families, most French-Canadian and Swiss, lived in scattered

1

2

3

Stone marker, site of the first Cathedral, Saint Paul

cabins stretching from Seven Corners to Lake Phalen. Many were fur traders and voyageurs working for the American Fur Company at Mendota. Women midwives served the needs of the growing settlement as well as those at Fort Snelling. Some Irish, Danes, an African-American, and the Dakota from near-by Kaposia added to the diversity of the frontier settlement. At the time much of the St. Paul settlement was under the jurisdiction of the diocese of Milwaukee while the rest of the territory, including Mendota and the settlement near the Falls of St. Anthony, still belonged to the diocese of Dubuque. Bishop Loras had sent Rev. Augustine Ravoux to replace Galtier as missionary into the Minnesota area. Ravoux visited Little Crow's Sioux village in Kaposia, wrote and published a catechism in the Lakota language, and served the Catholics in St. Paul, Mendota, Lake Pepin, St. Croix, and St. Anthony where he later erected a church in 1849.

In 1848 Minnesota achieved territorial status with its attendant governmental apparatus. Statehood would be the next stage of development. Bishop Loras of Dubuque petitioned Rome to create a new diocese for the growing population north of Iowa. Thus the Diocese of St. Paul became a reality in 1850, with Bishop Joseph Cretin named its first bishop. Once treaties were secured with the Indians in the region and the territory became opened by the U.S. government, immigrants began to flood into the state from East Coast states as well as directly from countries in Europe where various factors contributed to the great 19th century immigration. Vast numbers of immigrants from European countries found their way into the young United States and marked the Catholic Church in America as an "immigrant Church" with all the ethnic overtones that name suggests. This would also influence the development of the Church in the Minnesota Territory.

A papal decree issued July 19,1850 created the Diocese of St. Paul and appointed Joseph Cretin, Vicar General of Dubuque at the time, as first bishop. The diocese extended from Lake Superior to the Missouri River and from Iowa to the Canadian border. At the time it listed a population of about 3,000.

Early view of Saint Paul

Early view of St. Anthony Falls

Bishop Joseph Cretin

instructor there. In 1838 he came to the Dubuque diocese, imbued with enthusiasm to be a missionary in this vast new land. After his appointment as bishop of St. Paul, he arrived at the frontier settlement on July 2, 1851, was met by a group of eager citizens and escorted by Father Ravoux to his cathedral, the log chapel on Bench Street which Ravoux had enlarged. The Bishop's primitive shanty residence stood nearby. A large stone marker near today's Kellogg and Robert Streets memorializes St. Paul's first Cathedral.

JOSEPH CRETIN was born in Montluel, France where he was ordained in Belley and studied at the seminary of St. Sulpice and at Meximieux where he had been influenced by Bishop Loras, an

Severe challenges for the new bishop lay before him. St. Paul was but a small village and river port newly reclaimed from Minnesota's wilderness. Diocesan church buildings consisted of log structures in St. Paul, Mendota, St. Anthony and Pembina. Clerical personnel numbering Father Ravoux at St. Peter's in Mendota and Fathers Belcourt and Lacombe at Pembina way to the northwest, served a Catholic population of about 1000 amidst a total population in the entire region of 30,000

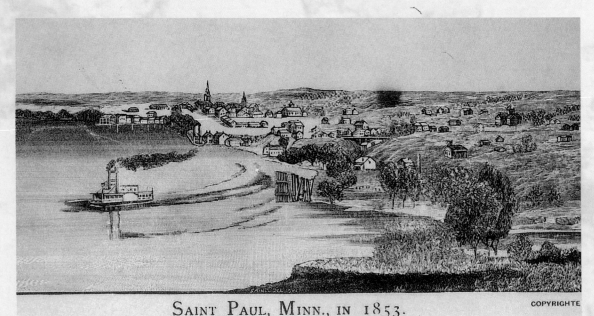

SAINT PAUL, MINN., IN 1853.

Catholic Cathedral.

Upper Levee.   Episcopal Church.   Simpson's Dwelling.   Baptist Church.   Phalen Creek.
Steamboat Landing.   Court House.   Prince's Saw Mill.   Capitol Building.
De Neill's Church   Bridge Cor. E. Fourth and Jackson Sts.

Chapel at Mendota, 1840s

Indians and 6,000 whites. The see was centered in the heart of a fur-trading operation. Business came by steamboat from the South and ox carts brought furs from the North. Immigrants came with the provisions from the South, thus making St. Paul quite a business center for the surrounding territory by 1851. Cretin met his new challenges by living his motto," All things to all men," as an example of the personal sacrifice and self-denial that would exemplify his style of leadership. His example was noted by young men who also wished to serve the church in this region.

With visions of establishing a seminary in his new diocese, Cretin recruited young clerics from France for seminary training under his supervision in St. Paul. In 1853

he sent Father Ravoux to France to place two St. Paul recruits, John Ireland and Thomas O'Gorman, in the preparatory seminary of Meximieux and to bring back other seminarians to St. Paul. Seven came. A newly combined church, residence, and school on Wabasha and Sixth streets became the new cathedral, episcopal see, and seminary for the diocese.

St. Peter's Church, Mendota

Main entrance of
St. Joseph's Academy
for girls, Saint Paul

"*Christ, the Lord, set up in his church a variety of offices which aim at the good of the whole body, so that all who belong to the People of God, and are endowed with true Christian dignity, may attain to salvation.*"

Lumen Gentium

Sisters of St. Joseph and Young Women, St. Joseph's Academy

In 1851 when the bishop moved to the new residence, the old log chapel on Bench Street became a school for girls under the direction of the Sisters of St. Joseph of Carondelet. These sisters came from St. Louis at the request of Cretin to organize the first school for girls in the Northwest, St. Joseph's Academy.

Lay entrepreneurs and developers in the area were eager that such an enterprise be undertaken. Later, as more room was needed, a new building for the academy was erected at Virginia and Nelson (later Marshall) Streets. This building also served as Motherhouse and Novitiate for the Sisters of St. Joseph in the St. Paul Province.

Bishop Cretin was also actively involved in the building of the first hospital in Minnesota. Laymen led by Doctor Daly, a physician of the village, procured land and provisions for construction of a hospital in 1851. Unable to see the project through, he sold the entire enterprise to Bishop Cretin who contributed personal funds to the hospital's completion in 1854. The Sisters of St. Joseph were placed in charge of the institution and provided a record of unselfish and dedicated service in the care of the sick during the cholera epidemic of 1855-1856. Before the hospital was completed, the Sisters cared for the sick in the old log building on Bench Street. Many of the cholera victims arrived on the river boats and had to be segregated immediately. Besides operating St. Joseph's hospital in St. Paul, the sisters were also to administer St. Mary's Hospital in Minneapolis for over 100 years.

Assumption church, Saint Paul, 1874

Church of St. Antony, Minneapolis, 1898

13

St. Joseph's Hospital, early 1900s

Missionary work among the Indian tribes in his see remained a primary concern of Bishop Cretin. He sent a priest to serve the Winnebagoes in Long Prairie. A Sister of St. Joseph accompanied Canon de Vivaldi in order to prepare the children for the reception of the sacraments. Because the Indians through treaty were considered wards of the federal government, Cretin sought help from the federal government but met strong opposition from Protestant groups throughout the country. Anti-Catholicism of the Know-Nothing Movement was strong in pre-Civil War America, so federal funds simply were not available for any social works sponsored by the St. Paul diocese.

Financial chaos plagued the Long Prairie school and mission and by 1856 the entire operation was abandoned. The government's flawed policy of using the Church to "civilize the savages" contributed to bad feelings between the Indians and the whites in the region, and provoked a long series of wars between the Indians and the federal army from 1862 until 1893.

Church of St. Margaret,
Minnetonka, 1849

> " . . . *Its citizens, who are taken from all nations,*
> *are of a kingdom whose nature is not only*
> *earthly but heavenly.*"
>
> *Lumen Gentium*

Cretin saw that the crying need of his young diocese was an increase of Catholic population so he undertook steps to bring immigrants to the area. Through letters written to Eastern and European papers, he encouraged immigration to the West. With the Treaty of Traverse des Sioux, vast tracts of Indian lands were opened to white settlement and immigrants came, including Catholics. Increasing numbers of French, Irish, and Germans took up lands along the Mississippi, Minnesota, and St. Croix Rivers. Prosperous settlements developed throughout the diocese.

In 1853, because the German population of St. Paul had grown so rapidly, Cretin authorized Rev. Michael Wirtzfeld to organize a German parish in St. Paul. The cornerstone of the original Church of the Assumption was laid in 1855 and Father Keller who spoke both German and English became the first pastor. Shortly thereafter, Benedictines took over the pastorship of the Assumption parish. In 1856 three Benedictines came from Latrobe, Pennsylvania, to help with the increased German population of Stearns County. They settled in St. Cloud, opened St. John's Seminary, and in 1856 moved permanently to Collegeville. Eventually St. John's was elevated to the rank of an Abbey with the Right Rev. Rupert Seidenbusch as first Abbot. This Abbey would become renowned for its leadership in liturgical reform and ecumenical endeavors during the development of the Catholic Church in America.

St. John's Abbey
Collegeville,
1940

Bishop Cetin was an itinerant pastor of parishes scattered throughout the vast territory that his see encompassed. Besides attending to his own Cathedral parish, he celebrated Mass, preached, and confirmed in Faribault, Fort Ripley, Belle Prairie, Mankato, Caledonia, Winona, Rochester, and Pembina. As early as 1852 he founded the Minnesota branch of the Catholic Temperance Society, encouraging all Catholics over the age of 12 to take the pledge against demon rum. He strove to have the Territorial Legislature pass a law making the manufacture, possession, or sale of liquor a penal offense subject to severe punishment. However, strong opposition in the diocese came from distillers and the growing German population. He supported a strong temperance program for the diocese throughout his entire term as bishop.

Ever conscious of his role as servant, Cretin founded the St. Joseph Conference of the St. Vincent de Paul Society to aid the poor and to enhance the spiritual life of the members by visiting the sick and the destitute. He supported the decrees of the First Plenary Council of Baltimore in 1852 in devising programs to counteract heresy and paganism. He ardently endeavored to convert the Indians in the territory to the Catholic Church.

Father Augustine Ravoux

Chalice attributed to Ravoux

On July 27, 1856 Cretin officiated at the laying of the cornerstone of St. Paul's Third Cathedral on the corner of Sixth and St. Peter Streets. That same year Calvary Cemetery, near Front and Dale Streets, was purchased and the bodies of the dead were transferred from the old Catholic cemetery to the new. The old cemetery had been on the site where the new St. Joseph's Academy was built. This ghoulish procedure of exhumation and transfer provided grist for many ghostly tales subsequently woven into the early history of the Academy.

Bishop Cretin did not live to see the completion of his new cathedral. After several months of illness, he died of edema in St. Paul on Feb. 22, 1857. After services in his cathedral, his body was interred in Calvary Cemetery. The affairs of the diocese were administered by Father Augustin Ravoux during the two year interval before another bishop came to St. Paul. In addition to the many apostolic works begun, the legacy of Bishop Cretin to the Church in the upper Mid-west included 29 churches, 35 stations, and 20 priests serving a Catholic population of about 50,000. Noble endeavors to convert the various Indian tribes to Catholicism soon took a secondary role to the services rendered to the growing needs of the

Devotional crucifix of Father Ravoux

immigrant Catholics settling the region. Dedicated religious men and women had begun to establish regional headquarters in the Diocese in order to assist in the charitable works so needed among the immigrant throngs. From the very beginning of the diocese, lay leadership had been evident in collaborating with the clergy and religious in addressing the needs of the growing church, especially the needs of the poor and in establishing benevolent societies to provide aid in times of exigencies. Economic, political, and social bigotry in the young United States excluded Catholics as ineligible recipients of the public charities.

During the interval when the diocese was without a bishop Father Augustin Ravoux served as administrator of the diocese. Many new parishes were established. Benedictines took over Assumption Parish and St. Mark's in Shakopee was established. St. Boniface in St. Anthony, St. Felix in Wabasha, Guardian Angels in Hastings, Guardian Angels in Chaska, and a new church at Marysburg demonstrated the growth of the Catholic church in the region. Ravoux also kept good relations with the Sioux and gave them good service during their ordeal after the Indian Uprising of 1862. Thirty-three of the 38 condemned Sioux chose Ravoux as their spiritual advisor when their death sentence was announced. He baptized 31 of the condemned prisoners before their execution. Ravoux held the honored position of Vicar General of the diocese under the next two prelates, Grace and Ireland, until 1892 when illness began to hamper his apostolic works. He died at St. Joseph's Hospital in 1906.

Early log chapel at Hastings

> **"***T*he holders of office, who are invested with sacred power, are, in fact dedicated to promoting the interests of all.***"**
>
> *Lumen Gentium*

Bishop Thomas L. Grace

THOMAS LANGDON GRACE, a native of South Carolina, was installed as second Bishop of St. Paul on July 29, 1859. He accepted his appointment to the St. Paul Diocese only reluctantly. Coming from an affluent, well-educated, and prestigious family, Grace joined the Dominican Order and after ordination taught at St. Rose Seminary in Pennsylvania. After serving the church for a time in Memphis, Tennessee, he came to his new see with a penchant for orderly administration, forward-looking educational values, and sound theological training for future priests. Grace devised a Constitution for the Diocese, stipulating what priests could and could not do regarding the celebration of the Eucharist, administration of the sacraments, upholding the decrees of the Baltimore Councils, erection of parish buildings, teaching children the rudiments of Catholicism, and the keeping of parish records.

Bishop Grace's pectoral cross

In 1860 Bishop Grace began constructing a more commodious residence adjoining the cathedral on Sixth Street. This would serve as the

Second Cathedral of Saint Paul

Early Cathedral School, Saint Paul, 1882

bishop's residence until the early 1890s when his successor, Archbishop Ireland, moved to 977 Portland Ave. before the completion of the rectory adjacent to the present cathedral building.

Setting a high priority, Grace strove to gain worthy and well-educated recruits for the priestly ranks for his diocese. In 1860 his first ordination to the priesthood included Edward Essing and Pius Bayer. The following year he ordained Rev. John Ireland in the uncompleted cathedral. Ireland, who had just returned from his studies in France, said his first Mass there. In 1865 he ordained James Trobec and Thomas O'Gorman, both of whom would become bishops of suffragan sees under Archbishop Ireland.

In 1860, Grace formed the Young Catholic Educational Society in his Cathedral Parish for the purpose of raising funds for the education of poor boys for the priesthood. Just two years later he opened the Educational Preparatory Seminary of St. Paul on the second floor of the old cathedral building with William Markoe in charge.

This school eventually merged with the Cathedral School about the same time that the Benedictines founded St. John's College in 1867. Students interested in becoming priests were sent there and to other seminaries for their theological training.

Minnesota became a state in 1858, just as Bishop Grace became acclimated to his new see. The succession of events that plummeted the states into the bloody Civil War caused additional pressures for the new diocesan prelate of this newest Northern state. Coming from South Carolina and knowing well the grievances of that section of the country, Grace's loyalties were severely tested. The grievances of the Indians in the territories of his diocese erupted in the bloodbath of the Sioux Uprising of 1862, exacerbating the horrors of the civil strife and testing the bishop's diplomatic skills both on the national and local scenes. The young Father Ireland went to serve as a chaplain for the North in battles fought on Southern soil. Health reasons brought him back to St. Paul where he eventually became secretary to Bishop Grace.

It was during the 1860s that the Mdwakanton Sioux at the Lower Sioux Agency in Minnesota asked Bishop Grace to send a "clergyman of the order of the black gowns" to be stationed among them and to see to the education of their children. They wanted a priest to serve as an agent of the federal government in their midst so that treaty rights of the Indians would be guaranteed. Correspondence between Grace and the Bureau of Indian Affairs did nothing to change U.S. government policies with the Indians. Indian removal to reservations in the West continued and Bishop Grace refused to be any part of the government's ill-conceived plan to subdue the tribes.

While Catholic immigrants to Minnesota signified tremendous growth in numbers for the Catholic Church in America, cultural differences among these newcomers posed serious problems for church leaders. Irish prelates dominated the American hierarchy and other ethnic groups voiced desires to have bishops over them who

were of their cultural background. Thousands of Irish migrated to the Northwest. The Irish Emigration Society encouraged many Irish from the old sod as well as from the congested areas of cities in the Eastern states to come to the rich farmlands of the West amid the woodlands and lakes of Minnesota. Various publications lured poverty-stricken throngs to seek new fortunes in the Minnesota area. In the 1870s the Irish Catholic Colonization Association was organized in Chicago under the auspices of the American Catholic hierarchy to further the growth of the Catholic Church in the region. While Grace was ardently involved in this organization, it was John Ireland who later became famous for ventures that would result in establishing almost totally Irish settlements in Minnesota.

German immigration to the region had been generated by the political hardships among the petty principalities in Central Europe after the demise of Napoleon. The German language held the disparate groups who came here in

Students from St. Lawrence School, Minneapolis

School of St. Joseph, Minneapolis, 1900

some kind of cultural unity. For German Catholics the retention of the German language would remain at the heart of their cultural identity well into the twentieth century. Leaders in this group demanded a German press, German-speaking priests and bishops, and school policies that would guarantee that the German language would live on in the immigrants' offspring. St. Paul Germans wanted not only their own ethnic parish church led by German clergy, and schools wherein instruction would be in German, but they also wanted their own cemetery for German-Catholics. They organized the St. Joseph Aid Society, purchased land near Randolph and Hamline for that purpose, but their intent for land usage was changed under Grace's direction. This property became the site of St. Joseph's Orphanage, staffed by the Benedictine Sisters. Polish and Italian groups in the city were also demanding clergy of their specific nationalities. Bishop Grace opposed this tendency to

St. Elizabeth's School, Minneapolis

staff the Church of America with bishops and priests of foreign extraction committed to a nationalizing policy. He was concerned that all Catholics be accepted as loyal Americans by the dominant Protestant groups in society. Feelings against Catholics and suspicions about their cultural programs ran high as America was struggling to define herself during the mid-19th century.

21

House of the Good Shepherd, Saint Paul, 1868

St. Elizabeth's Church, Minneapolis

The development of the Catholic press in the diocese received great encouragement from Bishop Grace. Shortly after the Civil War Father John Ireland proposed that a Catholic newspaper be founded in St. Paul. Under the leadership of John Crosby Devereux, *The Northwestern Chronicle* became the Catholic weekly. In 1867 under the leadership of the Benedictine Fathers of the Assumption Church, German Catholics launched *Der Wanderer* which printed some columns in the German language until the 1930s. A French weekly newspaper, *Le Canadien,* founded by M. D. Michaud appeared in 1877 and continued until 1903 when it merged with French publications out of Chicago. The Irish had *The Northwest Standard* (later changed to *The Irish Standard*) to defend the interests of the

Irish-Americans who were insulted by America's bigoted press. This was a national weekly, printed in English, which aimed to guard the sacred interests of the Catholic Church and to assist labor in its war against capital. The trend of immigrant groups to have their own papers and periodicals was followed by newer immigrants as they found their way to America.

Bishop Grace welcomed additional groups of sisters into the diocese to help with the needs of the growing Catholic community. In 1865 the Sisters of St. Dominic of Sinsinawa, Wisconsin took charge of the Immaculate Conception school in Faribault and soon opened Bethlehem Academy for girls. In 1868 Grace asked the Sisters of the Good Shepherd to establish a home for wayward girls in St. Paul. After attempting several locations, they finally erected Mount Eudes in 1883 on Blair and Milton. This became their Provincial House in the Northwest. Later they would move their facility to Hodgson Road in North Oaks. In 1873 Sisters of the Visitation arrived, settling first in Lower Town and eventually erecting a convent and academy at Grotto and Fairmount with the help of a daughter of James J. Hill. After WWII the sisters would move their complex to West St. Paul. The low status of women in American society during the greater part of the 19th century was reflected in the stance taken by Bishop Grace and indeed the entire American Church. Grace openly opposed the participation of women in political, civil, and national organizations no matter how worthy the cause. He openly discouraged the formation of women's leagues that were promoted by feminine leaders at the time. He claimed that their proper place was in the home. The sisterhoods that provided education for the young women truly paved the way for changing feminine thought toward more active roles in society for women.

Young Women at House of the Good Shepherd, Saint Paul, 1880

"*The Church, like a stranger in a foreign land, presses forward amid the persecutions of the world and the consolations of God.*"

Lumen Gentium

Cretin High School, Downtown, Saint Paul

It was during Grace's episcopate that Pope Pius IX issued the Syllabus of Errors which put the American Catholic Church on the defensive more than before. The syllabus reiterated the Church's condemnation of the evils of atheism, rationalism, indifferentism, socialism, communism, freemasonry, and various kinds of religious liberalism. Many Protestant leaders regarded this decree as a denunciation of their various sects and the American Protestant ethic which they held to be the very basis of American culture. A barrage of criticism against everything Catholic ensued, filling newspapers and periodicals with articles against Catholicism. The Second Plenary Council of Baltimore in 1866 affirmed the pope's decree and American bishops pledged to implement the Syllabus in their dioceses. Bishop Grace did his part in St. Paul. His penchant for orderly administration resulted in establishing deaneries throughout the diocese to implement the directives of the Vatican. Shortly after this, Rome convened Vatican Council I. Because of illness, Bishop Grace sent Father Ireland to represent him. The Council adjourned before completing its deliberations because of the political

troubles in Rome that resulted in making the pope a prisoner of the Vatican. However, the document on the infallibility of the pope had been issued, causing more negative reaction against the Church and the pope among American Protestants. In St. Paul, the bishop and diocesan priests led a rally at the Cathedral wherein immigrant Catholic groups protested the plundering of Church property in Italy. In America all of this turmoil contributed to the growing agitation for establishing stricter laws demanding separation of Church and State, particularly when Catholic leaders strove for financial aid for the struggling parochial schools. The plea of Catholic parents that they were being doubly taxed for educating their children according to conscience fell on deaf ears in the American courts.

Nevertheless, Grace's work in Catholic education continued. In 1871 he summoned the Christian Brothers to take charge of the Cathedral School for boys. This venture evolved into Cretin High School on St. Peter and Main Streets. In 1882 there were 12 Christian Brothers teaching the older boys while the younger ones were under the care of

the Sisters of St. Joseph. In 1928 the new Cretin High School would be established at Hamline and Randolph Streets. There was also an abortive attempt to start a Catholic Industrial School on the property where The University of St. Thomas now stands. This school floundered in St. Paul, moved to Swift County as a school for Indian and white boys, and finally closed in 1879.

Brother Ambrose,
Director, Cretin High School

"*In the person of the bishops, then to whom the priests render assistance, the Lord Jesus Christ, supreme high priest, is present in the midst of the faithful.*"

Lumen Gentium

As more Catholics migrated to the diocese, more parishes were established and church construction proliferated during the 1860s. Most of these buildings served the rural areas in Minnesota, attesting to the increasing numbers of immigrants coming to rural Minnesota as well as to the metropolitan area. On June 29, 1871 the first consecration of a church in the diocese took place at Clinton (later St. Joseph) Minnesota. In 1875 the Vicariate of Northern Minnesota was established with the Right Rev. Rupert Seidenbusch, O.S.B.

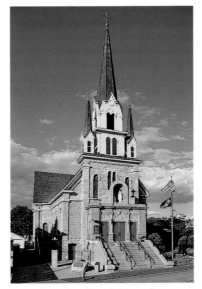

Our Lady of Lourdes,
Minneapolis

consecrated as the Vicar Apostolic of the new territory with residence in St. Cloud. That same year John Ireland became coadjutor to Bishop Grace with the right of succession. When word reached Bishop Grace that his petition for Ireland to be made his coadjutor had been honored, he was in Lourdes, France. He vowed that the next church in his diocese would be placed under the protection of Our Lady of Lourdes. The Notre Dame de Lourdes Church was organized in Northeast Minneapolis in 1877. French Catholics in St. Anthony gravitated toward

St. Anthony of Padua, Minneapolis

this parish. In Lower Town St. Paul Germans got permission to found a parish exclusively for themselves. Thus in 1881 the parish of the Sacred Heart on Dayton's Bluff was founded. Ethnic parishes proliferated as more immigrants came to the area. When the Vicariate of North Dakota was created in 1879 and Right Reverend Martin Marty, O.S.B. became its first bishop, the diocese of St. Paul became focused on the southern half of the state of Minnesota.

Annual priest's retreat, 1870

PHOTOGRAPH TAKEN AT THE ANNUAL RETREAT, 1870

Bishop Grace was one of the earliest and staunchest advocates of establishing a Catholic University for America. In 1880 he encouraged Bishop John Spalding of Peoria to go ahead with his proposal, finally accepted at the Third Plenary Council of Baltimore, and approved by Pope Leo XIII. The university became a reality in 1889 when formal classwork began at Catholic University in Washington, D.C. Grace's interest in this venture stemmed from his cherished wish to establish a major seminary under his own control in his own diocese. His plans for establishing St. Thomas Aquinas Seminary on lands now occupied by the University of St. Thomas became a reality on March 7, 1886, when he assisted at the High Mass inaugurating the opening of the seminary at that location.

In 1884, just a week after the celebration of his Silver Jubilee as bishop, Grace publicly resigned as Bishop of the St. Paul Diocese in favor of his coadjutor, John Ireland. The diocese was raised to archepiscopal status in 1888 with Ireland the first archbishop. At that time Grace was also elevated to archepiscopal rank as Titular Archbishop of Siunia. Bishop Grace died at St. Joseph's Hospital in St. Paul in 1897. His legacy to the diocese was that of a leader who believed in planning for the future. He was a prelate of brilliant intellectual attainments, knowledgeable about religious trends and tendencies in America and Europe. He was a linguist, had a good business head, demonstrated dignity and gentility, and was known for his concern for the poor and needy. A capable administer, he added stability to a rapidly growing immigrant Church in Minnesota and the Northwest.

"For the bishops... are authentic teachers, endowed with the authority of Christ, who preach the faith to the people assigned to them, the faith which is destined to inform their thinking and direct their conduct."

Lumen Gentium

Bishop John Ireland

St. Mary's
Church,
Lowertown,
Saint Paul

JOHN IRELAND was born in County Kilkenny, Ireland, in 1838 and migrated to America in 1850. Staying for a time in New York, then Vermont and Illinois, the Irelands decided to make their home in the northwest. Coming by steamer, they landed in St. Paul, May 20, 1852, and built a home in that frontier village. The young Ireland became a protege of Bishop Cretin who guided his training for the priesthood, eventually sending him to France where Ireland pursued his seminary studies at Meximieux and at the Marist Scholasticate at Montbel. He returned to St. Paul and was ordained by Bishop Grace on December 22, 1861, when the country was torn apart with civil strife. He saw action as a chaplain at the Battle of Corinth in 1862.

After serving for a brief time as army chaplain, Ireland returned to his diocese as secretary to Bishop Grace. In 1867 he served as pastor of St. Mary's parish in Lower Town and in 1875 was appointed coadjutor to Bishop Grace. For more than half a century, Ireland was a dominant figure in the religious, social, and political life of the United States. This was an era when the nation enjoyed tremendous industrial growth and

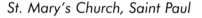

international importance. Ireland's episcopacy proved him a man of vision and daring, a patriot whose loyalty to his country was second only to his love for God and the Church. Church property in St. Paul at the time of Ireland's installation, included seven churches — Cathedral, Assumption, St. Mary's, St. Stanislaus, St. Michael's, St. Louis, and St. Joseph's — and five other institutions operated by women religious. These included St. Joseph's Academy, the House of the Good Shepherd, Catholic Orphanage, St. Joseph's Hospital, and the Visitation Academy. The diocese would grow tremendously through the colonization activities of the new bishop.

Ireland launched the Irish Immigration Society, encouraging settlers beset by economic poverty in

Archbishop Ireland's pectoral cross

their homeland to come to Minnesota and establish new homes and find opportunities to better their standard of living in America. The movement was put on a national basis, appealing to immigrants of all nationalities. By 1880 the society had settled numerous families in Minnesota, either on government or railroad land: 800 families in Swift County, 400 in Big Stone and Traverse, 300 in Nobles, 200 in Murray, and 70 in Lyons. So many immigrants came that the host American society feared their influence on the established structures of American society. Catholics especially were suspect since old prejudices were difficult to overcome. The Roman pontiff again became a pariah for Protestant America.

St. Mary's Church, Saint Paul

1

1. Women religious ministering to orphans in Saint Paul

2. Orphan Asylum, Saint Paul, 1886

3. Sisters of St. Joseph Orphan Asylum, Saint Paul

4. Benedictine Sisters' St. Joseph's Orphanage, Saint Paul

5. Catholic Orphan Asylum, Minneapolis, 1878

2

3

4

5

St. Mary's Hospital, Minneapolis

"*The college or body of bishops has for all that no authority unless united with the Roman Pontiff, Peter's successor, as its head, whose primatial authority over all, whether pastors or faithful, remains in its integrity.*"

Lumen Gentium

When Ireland became Bishop of St. Paul on July 31, 1884, the Catholic population was about 130,000. The diocese listed 147 priests, 119 diocesan and 28 regular clergy. There were 195 churches and 51 stations, 29 seminarians, 6 religious communities of men, 14 religious communities of women, 2 hospitals, 5 asylums, 10 academies and boarding schools for young women. There were seven St. Vincent de Paul Conferences, Total Abstinence Societies in many communities, rosary societies in most parishes as well as sodalities and confraternities of the Sacred Heart. By this time Ireland's reputation as an eloquent speaker had spread. His discourses and sermons were published in pamphlet form and in the *Northwestern Chronicle*. His work with colonization and temperance made him known beyond the Atlantic.

Holy Rosary Church, Minneapolis

Ireland made his mark of leadership at the Third Plenary Council of Baltimore in November, 1884. He preached in the Baltimore

Reverend Michael Harrigan, O.P., early pastor of Holy Rosary Church, Minneapolis

Cathedral on "The Catholic Church and Civil Society", stressing the teachings of the Catholic Church in relation to social authority and political liberty. He stressed the elements of patriotism demanded of all coming to America. He was a member of the group that spearheaded the founding of the United States Catholic Historical Society, stressing the importance of preserving the history of the Catholic church in America to show the compatibility of Catholicism with true American patriotism. In Minnesota he had long been an active member of the Minnesota State Historical Society, serving as president in 1877.

Under Ireland's leadership, the Total Abstinence Movement was recognized by the Third Plenary Council of Baltimore and also achieved approval from Rome. The movement pressured all Catholics to join and all parishes to encourage parishioners to take the pledge against the use of alcoholic beverages. Ireland was criticized for

30

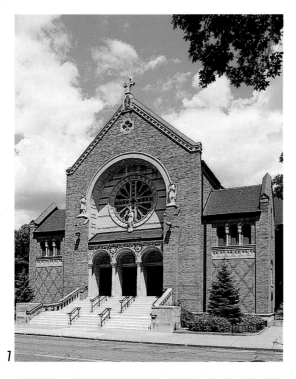

1

2

3

4

5

6

A sampling of the early ethnic churches of the Archdiocese.

1. St. Boniface, Minneapolis

2. Holy Cross, Minneapolis

3. St. Agnes, Saint Paul

4. St. Adalbert, Saint Paul

5. Altar in St. Mark, Saint Paul

6. Ascension, Minneapolis

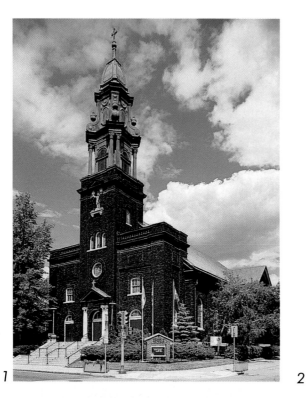

1. St. Cyril and
Methodius,
Minneapolis

2. Stained glass
window,
Joan of Arc,
St. Louis Church,

3. Stained glass
window,
King St. Louis,
St. Louis Church,

4. Assumption
Ceiling,
Saint Paul

5. Assumption,
Saint Paul

6.& 7 Angels and
stained glass
windows,
St. Maron

1

2

4

3

5

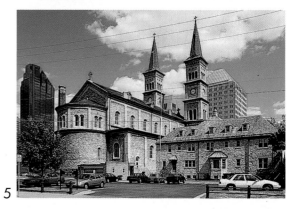

6

7

this radical stand on temperance by many central European immigrant groups, especially Germans. Some important German industrialists in Minnesota, especially the noted distillers, were unhappy with Ireland's crusade.

This movement fueled the fire of controversy between Ireland and the broader hyphenated-American community. There were debates between Ireland and ethnic groups who wanted to retain old-world customs and cultures, especially the use of their native languages, in being assimilated into America. Germans, especially the learned and politically astute forty-eighters, provided leadership in fighting Ireland's Americanism. Ireland's philosophy wedded patriotism to America with being a strong Catholic, demanding that ways of the old world must be shed in assuming true Americanism. This meant that foreign languages in civic affairs, in the marketplace, and in Church affairs be abandoned in preference to the English language, the tongue of the adopted country of the immigrants. Ireland feared that continued use of foreign tongues would bring grave criticism on the Catholic Church in America.

St. Paul's Germans were aided in their stance by the St. Raphael Verein, founded by Peter Paul Cahensly in 1883

Most Holy Redeemer Chapel (Lower level of 3rd Cathedral)

to provide for the spiritual welfare of foreign language groups, especially Germans, in the United States. This Verein had international support in promoting the formation of national parishes with priests of that nationality in charge, or at least with priests who would be strictly obliged to teach the truths of Catholicism in the language of the particular ethnic group comprising the parish. The Verein further advocated that parish schools be directed to teach the ethnic language, that ethnic societies be organized for the preservation of specific ethnic cultures, and that bishops of each ethnic group be provided to balance the overwhelmingly Irish character of the American hierarchy.

In 1886 the German clergy petitioned Rome for relief, claiming that it was a matter of saving souls since the faith could only be passed on within the context of the respective ethnic culture of an immigrant group. At the time Ireland and Keane of Richmond were in Rome pleading the cause of the Catholic University of America. They countered the German petition by saying that to grant the Germans their request would be disastrous to the Church in the United States. They denied that English-speaking bishops were discouraging the use of the German language or customs. They further warned that to bow to the wishes of the Germans would create

Assumption Church Girl's School, Saint Paul

1. St. Louis School, Saint Paul

2. Boys School, Assumption Parish, Saint Paul

3. St. Agnes School, 1880s

St. Michael's Church, Stillwater

chaos in prompting similar requests from other nationalities. The American church had within its fold multiple nationality groups. Rome's reply satisfied neither side. Rome declared that it would never direct bishops as in the German petition, but it would allow them to provide the best they could for immigrants in the matter of language. The controversy did not die but resulted in a rift between Ireland and ethnic groups in the diocese. Irish clergy blamed German hierarchy in Cincinnati, Milwaukee, and St. Louis for making an attempt to control Catholic affairs in America. Ireland's meddling in the internal election of a new abbot at St. John's Abbey did not help the situation. Throughout the controversy Ireland maintained that children must learn English well because English was the language of the country and must be given an honored place in the education of all American children. English as well as German must be the medium of Catholic instruction since English anti-Catholic statements must be answered in English in the defense of the faith.

Ireland's great concern was always that American Catholic children be trained in order to assume a competitive leadership role within the greater American society so that their Catholic philosophy might impact the mores of the emerging American culture. His Faribault School Plan was based on this premise. Bishop Grace's abortive plan to procure legislation giving state aid to sectarian schools notwithstanding, Ireland's attempt to ease the burden of double taxation for diocesan Catholics was much bolder. Parochial schools were finding it increasingly difficult to finance their operations. Immaculate Conception School in Faribault was Ireland's test case. The school, with its equipment and grounds, would be placed under the Board of Education in the county. The

Dominican sisters would be retained and their salaries and all expenses of administration would be paid out of public funds. It would thus be operating as part of the public school system, subject to the secular curriculum and examination standards. Religious instruction would be offered by the sisters only after the formal school day. The plan was accepted by the Faribault school board and became operative Aug. 31, 1891 with the name of the school being changed to "Hill School." The plan was also adopted in Stillwater with the Sisters of St. Joseph at St. Michael's School. Both schools flourished. Catholics were now able to provide more generously to parish needs. Parish debts were paid. Similar arrangements had been in effect in other parts of the country for many years.

St. Stephen's Church, Anoka

Opposition to Ireland's plan came from strong Protestant groups throughout the state. These claimed that this was surrender of public schools to the Catholic Church, "a clever trick of the Archbishop of St. Paul to capture the public schools for the Church of Rome." They claimed that the nuns would use the school to teach Catholic tenets. A Stillwater group threatened legal proceedings to revoke the contract between the parish and the school board. A group of Minneapolis ministers made a similar demand on the ground that the arrangement was a complete victory of the Catholic church over the State. Opposition also came from German Catholics who feared their schools would become discredited. They criticized Ireland for his "liberalism" in preaching about the right of the state to educate all children regardless of religious affiliation. They complained to Rome that Ireland was not complying with the decrees of the Plenary Council of Baltimore which promoted Catholic Schools and their need for the education of youth. The secular press took up the debate. Several Catholic writers championed Ireland's position as he went to Rome to defend his idea. Rome approved the operation of his plan only in these two schools. The controversy became national when the APA (American Protestant Association) used the school controversy to establish the principle of separation of church and state through subsequent state laws that resulted from national lobbying efforts. The issue triggered a barrage of anti-Catholic press propaganda throughout the country. Because of opposition, the Stillwater experiment was discontinued. That of Faribault died after two years when the school board substituted Protestant teachers for the sisters. Ireland, however, used his plan elsewhere. In Waverly, St. Mary's was a consolidated parochial and public school from 1893 to 1904, when it reverted to parochial status. At that point the Faribault Plan of Ireland's ceased altogether.

Ireland's support of the Paulist founder, Rev. Isaac Hecker, and his theory of Americanism brought him into opposition with some of the other bishops in America as well as church leaders abroad. Hecker postulated new methods of approach to non-Catholics, called for the adaptation of Catholic doctrine to the modern world both under the duly constituted authority of the church as well as personal compliance to inspiration of the Holy Spirit within individuals.

Students of St. Anthony School, Minneapolis, 1898

35

St. Mary's Church, Waverly

Ascension Parish School, 1853

Benson delegates to Total Abstinence Society Convention, Saint Paul

St. Adalbert's School, Saint Paul, 1880s

Ireland lauded Hecker's teaching regarding the submission of the individual soul to the guidance of the Holy Spirit and the need of active rather than passive virtues in meeting the religious conditions of the modern world. French clerics accused this "Americanism" as one of the greatest dangers facing the Church and

accused Ireland of supporting the heresy of modernism. The Church later condemned modernism in that it made divine truth nothing more than the speculative description of human feelings and interpreted the dogmas of faith as expressions of mere subjective experience. Ireland's writings proved that he was far removed from such thought. He twice went to Rome to correct Rome's misconception of Hecker's ideas. Although he had the support of a number of American bishops, others opposed his ideas. Archbishop Corrigan from the East Coast openly condemned some of Hecker's philosophy and other bishops, not wanting to alienate either bishop, became fence-sitters in the controversy. When Ireland was in Rome, he spoke glowingly of American Catholics and their loyalty to the church, but a church that wanted to be independent of any temporal power. Ireland also opposed Rome's condemnation of Catholics joining fraternal lodges, as the Knights of Pythias, Sons of Temperance, and Masonic Societies in that these were fraternal benevolent societies featuring life insurance, sick and death benefits and did not hold practices antagonistic to the church and her teachings. Later Rome would allow nominal membership in some of these groups, as long as the society would have nothing to do with the funeral of a Catholic member. Ireland's enemies claimed he had become secularized in his support of the notion of separation of Church and state. Cardinal Rampola assured Ireland that Leo XIII never intended to condemn the real Americanism that Ireland espoused, but the controversy played heavily against Ireland when later his name was recommended to Rome for elevation to the cardinalate. He was never to receive the red hat.

Archbishop Ireland had relied on his friendship with big business tycoons, not all Catholics, in the region, especially James J. Hill, in launching many of his programs for expansion of the church in his diocese. In 1896 these business contacts urged Ireland to depart from his rule of non-interference in purely political matters, by making public his opinions on the burning questions then before the electorate, especially the issue of free silver as proposed by the Democratic candidate, William Jennings Bryan. Big business opposed this idea and fought for hard money, the gold standard. Ireland came out in the Catholic press for hard money and actively supported the presidential campaign of William McKinley. Many farmers and industrial workers were swayed by Ireland's opinion. When the war hawks got the United States to the brink of war with Catholic Spain, Pope Leo XIII called on Ireland to act as his arbiter to avert the conflict. Ireland was too impulsive an activist to deal with the waffling president and a war-determined congress. His diplomatic venture failed to the displeasure of the Vatican. America

James J. Hill, railroad magnate and friend of Archbishop Ireland

went to war and demanded imperialistic gains in the treaty that followed.

Sisters of St. Joseph nurses serving U.S. soldiers in Cuba during the Spanish-American War

"The bishops, as vicars and legates of Christ, govern the particular Churches assigned to them."

Lumen Gentium

When the diocese of St. Paul was elevated to archiepiscopal status, new waves of immigrants from southern and eastern Europe added to the burgeoning Catholic population of the Northwest. Ireland called for the erection of new dioceses in the territory. In 1889 five new suffragan sees were erected: Sioux Falls in South Dakota; Fargo in North Dakota; and St. Cloud, Duluth, and Winona in Minnesota. Bishops McGolrick (Duluth), Cotter (Winona), and Shanley (Fargo) were consecrated by Ireland in a triple ceremony in the St. Paul Cathedral. Although the archdiocese comprised both rural and urban areas, by far the greater Catholic population was concentrating within the proximity of the expanding Twin Cities of St. Paul and Minneapolis with all of the attending problems that urban concentrations posed on an immigrant Church.

Ireland was an ardent advocate of lay participation in spreading Catholicism in America. At the First Lay Catholic Congress in Baltimore in 1889, 1500 delegates convened to pledge support to active lay ministries. 31 came from Minnesota: 23 from St. Paul, 2 from Minneapolis, and 6 from rural Minnesota. For the diocese, the most important outcome of the congress was the founding of the Catholic Truth Society in St. Paul, March 10, 1890. This was the first society of such a nature in the United States. Most of its tracts were of an apologetic nature. After five years, it merged with the International Catholic Truth Society of Brooklyn, New York.

Early St. Thomas College

Reverend John A. Ryan.

diocese served on the faculty, and many of St. Paul's clergy became recognized leaders of the institution. Probably Monsignor John Ryan, from the St. Paul Seminary, was the most distinguished of these for his work in expounding theories of social justice laid down in the papal social encyclicals of Leo XIII and Pius XI.

Considering the expansion of higher education for Catholics necessary for training Catholic leaders for American society, Ireland strove to establish a top-rated seminary, a Catholic men's college, and a Catholic women's college in St. Paul. Aided by the generosity of the railroad entrepreneur, James J. Hill, Ireland was able to open the St. Paul Seminary in 1894. The buildings and grounds given to the former St. Thomas Aquinas Seminary were converted into St. Thomas Academy and College for men. Ireland donated land to the Sisters of St. Joseph for the establishing of the College of St. Catherine for women. He hand picked the stalwart leader, Sister Antonia McHugh, C.S.J. to establish St. Catherine's under his shared philosophy of molding young Catholic women for leadership

Student Body, Saint Paul Seminary, 1900

From its founding, the Catholic University of America was of special concern to Ireland. As an member of the original board of governors, he hoped to map out the programs of the institution and guide its progress through years of struggle and expansion. He saw the university receive recognition from leading universities in the country, satisfying Ireland's philosophy of making all Catholic endeavors in American society truly competitive with non-Catholics in that society. From the beginning, students from the archdiocese were in attendance, scholarly priests of the

Father Anatole Oster, seminary spiritual director

roles in the American society of the new millennium. This was a daring venture when the role of women was subservient both in church and civic affairs.

But Ireland's pet project in higher education lay in establishing the St. Paul Seminary, made possible by the generous gift of James J. Hill, president of the Great Northern Railway. The money was to be used for building and endowing a seminary for the education of priests. The seminary was opened on September 6, 1894 with the Rt. Rev. Louis E. Caillet the first rector. Ireland drew up the Constitution and Rules for the Seminary, keeping the educational and spiritual matters in the hands of the Ordinary of the Diocese and exercising these in due conformity with the laws of the Church. His influence on the seminary was profound and he closely oversaw the development of its programs for 25 years. He wanted an intelligent and holy priesthood that would challenge a world estranged from God to make Christ live once more among humankind. Along with theology, Ireland encouraged the natural sciences as signs of the power of

God in the material order as Revelation spoke of His preeminence in the spiritual realm of life. Ireland was ahead of his times in his vision of the interdependence of the two. He was determined to make the St. Paul Seminary the leading institution in the country for the training of recruits for the priesthood in America. Ireland was also a great supporter of founding an American seminary for the education of priests for the foreign mission field. He became an ardent supporter and great friend of the seminary established at Maryknoll, New York. Through his efforts the Twin Cities became a recruiting center for foreign missionaries from the entire Northwest. The St. Paul Diocesan Society for the Propagation of the Faith served as a major benefactor for works of that society abroad.

Ireland's concern that Catholic education be on a par with that offered by secular society was ever uppermost in his

Archbishop John Ireland

thinking. In 1890 he organized an eight member Diocesan School Board to provide inspection of all Catholic schools in the diocese, test the children's progress, and supervise a unified curriculum. Although secular subjects would be taught, religious training, with the catechism and Bible history at the core of the curriculum, would ward against a secularization of Catholic students. Ireland convinced the National Catholic Educational Association to hold its annual convention in St. Paul in 1915. Of great concern to Ireland was the religious welfare of Catholic students at the University of Minnesota, with campuses in both cities. The Minneapolis campus had become known for its secularism and anti-Catholic outbursts. On March 18, 1903 Ireland organized the Students' Catholic Association, housed in the Y.M.C.A. building near the university. Later the name was changed to "Newman Center" and eventually procured its own building across from the university. In

1928 Newman Hall became the property of the archdiocese of St. Paul.

The continuing flow of immigrants, the expansion of the archdiocese, the depressions of 1873 and 1893 all added to the growing cries of the poor in the archdiocese. The bishops of the St. Paul Diocese had been known for their love of the poor and underprivileged. The continuous work of the St. Vincent de Paul Societies, in providing food, clothing, and other necessities to those in need was encouraged by Ireland during the hard times. He organized the Catholic Central Bureau in 1887 to provide for the floaters and transients who found their way into St. Paul. An office under the management of Lorenzo Markoe and Joseph Roupf was set up in the transept of the old cathedral to supply information to strangers and visitors and to give temporary relief to those not cared for by other agencies.

Ireland was also involved in organizing the National Conference of Catholic Charities which operated from 1909 to 1910.

Badge of the Catholic Educational Association Meeting, Saint Paul, 1915

Chinese converts, St. Vincent de Paul Church, Saint Paul

1. *St. Luke Church, Saint Paul*

2. *Window from St. Mark Church, Saint Paul*

3. *St. Vincent de Paul Church, Saint Paul*

4. *St. Peter Claver, Old Church*

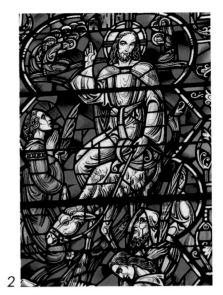

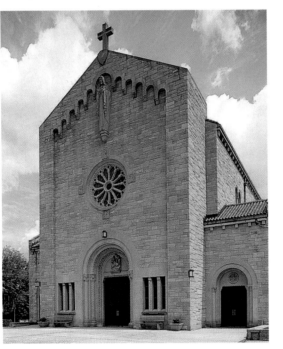

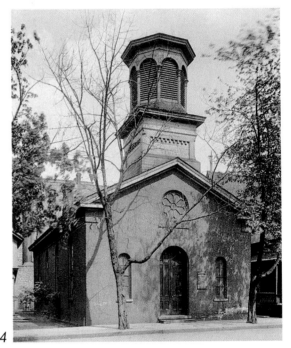

St. Peter Claver Congregational Choir

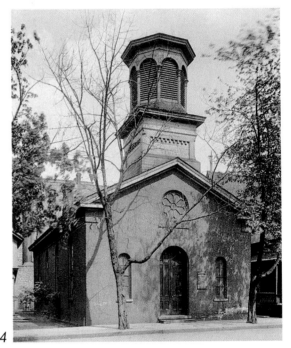

During this time Ireland appointed John R. Power, assistant pastor of St. Mary's Church to look after the Catholic children who came before him. He also arranged to have Power commissioned by the Juvenile Court as a probation officer.

The number of parishes in St. Paul listed in 1901 attests to the growth of urban Catholics under Ireland's hand. The list included:

St. Peter - 1840	St. Patrick -1884
Cathedral -1841	St. John -1886
St. Margaret - 1849	St. Mathew - 1886
St. Antony of Padua - 1849	St. James - 1887
St. John the Evangelist - 1852	St. Vincent - 1887
Assumption - 1856	St. Agnes - 1887
St. Mary - 1867	St. Luke - 1888
St. Stanislaus - 1872	St. Peter Claver - 1888
St. Michael - 1874	St. Mark -1889
St. Joseph -1875	St. Bernard - 1890
St. Adalbert - 1880	St. Casimir - 1893
Sacred Heart -1881	St. Andrew - 1896
St. Francis de Sales - 1884	Holy Redeemer - 1899

42

The year 1901 also marked the Golden Jubilee of the Diocese of St. Paul. Festivities included the celebration of a Pontifical Mass on the St. Paul Seminary grounds, presentation of a Jubilee Fund and Diocesan Album, the laying of the cornerstone of St. Mary's Chapel on St. Thomas College grounds, a grand parade of parish organizations and independent societies through downtown St. Paul, and a huge meeting in the St. Paul Auditorium in the evening of June 2, 1901. Ireland spoke on "Fifty Years of Catholicity in the Northwest" and the evening closed with the assembly singing the national anthem.

In 1904 Ireland began plans for the construction of a new cathedral building, the crowning achievement of his fruitful episcopate. At the time of

Celebration of the last Mass in the third Cathedral of Saint Paul

the 50th anniversary of the diocese, he indicated his great dream of the future. He saw a majestic cathedral dominating the skyline of his beloved city of St. Paul and also a majestic pro-cathedral erected for Minneapolis. For his cathedral, he chose the magnificent

Children watch as workers raise a stone cross to the top of the Cathedral

43

Cathedral
construction site

Basilica of St. Mary, Minneapolis, 1940's

site on the brow of what was known as St. Anthony Hill, procured the necessary land, and named E.L. Masqueray the architect. Not only did the Catholics of the area watch with wonderment the erection of the great building, but the entire citizenry of St. Paul awaited the completion of the domed structure that would hold such a dominant place in the skyline of the capital city. Following the Classical Renaissance style of architecture, the Cathedral was to be an adaptation of the original plan of St. Peter's in Rome but the floor plan was in the shape of a Greek cross. The cornerstone was laid on June 2, 1907 and the structure was dedicated April 11, 1915, although it was still unfinished. The substantial finishing of the interior would be left to Ireland's successor, Archbishop Austin Dowling. Interior decorating of the dome, huge mosaics of the cardinal virtues, and larger-than- life statues of the four evangelists would be undertaken in the 1950s when Monsignor George Ryan was rector of the Cathedral.

Derham Hall, the College of St. Catherine, Saint Paul

At the same time, work progressed in Minneapolis for a replacement of the stone structure of the Church of the Immaculate Conception. The site chosen was the commanding hill overlooking Hennepin Avenue. Work began June 21, 1905 with the purchase of land. On August 7, 1907 ground-breaking took place and the cornerstone was laid May 31, 1908. This pro-cathedral was dedicated in 1914 under the title of Mary, Mother of God. It was officially consecrated on June 27, 1941 and renamed the Basilica of St. Mary at that time. This period of fierce competition between St. Paul and Minneapolis for dominance in the state prompted discussion among civic leaders of the possibility of uniting the two cities into one municipality. Ireland favored this idea, until outsider publications belittled his precious city, St. Paul. The cities really wished to remain separate and Ireland championed his capital city throughout the rest of his life. Ireland's varied concerns kept him in the vanguard of religious and secular activities during the progressive period in America's evolution. As pastor of the Cathedral he used his oratory to win others to his ideas and to make important pronouncements that would impact American thinking far beyond his archdiocese. As a writer and apologist he stood in the front rank of American ecclesiastics. Writing for Catholics and non-Catholics alike, he

Our Lady of Victory Chapel, The College of St. Catherine, Saint Paul

Knights of Columbus pins

showed the harmony that exists between religion and the basic principles of the American Constitution. A collection of his most important essays and addresses reached a world-wide audience under the title, *The Church and Modern Society*. Profits from the sales of this book were given toward the establishment of the College of St. Catherine for women. In 1905 Ireland organized the Catholic Historical Society with the intention of collecting all kinds of materials relating to Catholic development, not only in the the St. Paul area, but in the entire Northwest. In 1913 the official title became "The Catholic Historical Society of St. Paul" and the society's official organ was *Acta et Dicta*. The society became inactive when Ireland died, was revived in 1932 under Archbishop Murray and had periodic publications until 1936.

Ireland helped organize the St. Paul Council of the Knights of Columbus February 22, 1899. This was the first council west of Chicago. The Knights erected a club house on Smith Avenue, later to become the Catholic Youth Center of St. Paul. The oath taken by the knights was a pledge of loyalty to Church and to country, which resonated entirely with Ireland's philosophy of promoting dedicated American-Catholic activism.

Until the time of his death Ireland remained influential in national politics. His counsel was actively sought by men of prominence in every walk of life, especially leaders in the Republican Party who savored his influence with immigrant throngs of the electorate. When the Prohibition Amendment was debated throughout the country, Ireland spoke out against it, although he had been a major champion of prohibition for most of his adult life. He feared that the passing of the amendment would lull the advocates of total abstinence into such a security that the crusade against the use of liquor would become a thing of the past. Washington legislators recognized Ireland's ability to ascertain the trends of the times and to promote workable courses of action to sway public opinion. During a time when issues of Church/State controversies reached congressional levels, Ireland used his political ability to forestall much legislation that would have been detrimental to the welfare of the Church.

Ireland became ill during 1917 and he was never able to regain his strength. His physical condition deteriorated throughout 1918 and death came on September 25, 1918, shortly after his 80th birthday. His funeral Mass was celebrated in his beloved Cathedral amid much pomp on October 2, 1918. He was buried in Calvary Cemetery, next to his predecessors, Cretin and Grace.

Ireland's episcopacy in St. Paul had been marked by the expansion that had characterized the civic community during the last three decades of the 19th century and the first 20 years of the 20th century. This legacy of growth contributed to a remarkably visible institutional Catholic Church in the Midwest. During these years the number of diocesan priests increased from 130 to 302; priests of religious orders from 29 to 56; churches with resident pastors from 117 to 208; parochial schools from 63 to 102; pupils in these schools from 11, 748 to 25,730; seminarians from 160 to 210; academies for girls from 4 to 10 with 2,597 pupils. Enrollment at the College of St. Thomas was 1,050; at the College of St. Catherine it was 354. There were 1,200 sisters of different religious communities in the Archdiocese.

46

The status of women, blacks, and other minorities was given oratorical encouragement, but in reality, the level of prestige these groups enjoyed in the archdiocese was on a par with the low status of these groups generally throughout the country. Most of the lay groups organized during the Ireland years enhanced the role of lay men. Work enhancing the role of women in the archdiocese was furthered by women religious, who had to struggle with obtaining diocesan permissions in order to accomplish their missions for the Church. Little recognition was ever extended to the women who performed these works of service. The hierarchical Church was very slow to make any changes in this regard, even into the middle of the 20th century.

Archbishop Ireland's funeral procession, 1918

47

AUSTIN DOWLING was appointed second Archbishop of the Diocese of St. Paul in January, 1919. Serving as Bishop of Des Moines, Iowa since 1912, Dowling reluctantly accepted his new appointment. He was a New Englander, born of Irish immigrants who settled in New York and then Newport, Rhode Island. Dowling was an educator and a capable administrator. One of his first actions was to provide for the supervision of the 93 parochial schools in his diocese. He appointed Rev. James A. Byrne of the St. Paul Seminary as first Superintendent of the Archdiocesan Bureau of Education, under which the elementary and secondary schools of the diocese have functioned ever since.

Archbishop Austin Dowling

In February, 1919 the new Archbishop gave his approval and blessing to the newly formed Minnesota Council of Catholic Women, comprised of delegates from Catholic women's groups throughout the state. Later he encouraged the formation of the Archdiocesan Council of Catholic Men under the title "Twin Cities School of Social Studies," which was committed to further Catholic education by presenting the truths of faith to the laity in a pleasing and instructive manner. This group functioned for a time and went out of existence in the mid-1920s.

In the latter part of September, 1919 the first annual meeting of the American hierarchy was held at the Catholic University in Washington. Dowling was one of the 93 archbishops and bishops who attended. The deliberations of the bishops resulted in the formation of the National Catholic Welfare Conference. This voluntary association of members of the hierarchy would strive to take common counsel of matters of general import for the welfare of the church in the United States. Through a spirit of cooperation members would strive to serve and promote Catholic unity. They agreed to further religious and social welfare of the Church in America, aid the Catholic press, promote Catholic publicity, and assist home and foreign mission work. Archbishop Dowling served on the administrative board of the Conference. As chair of the the Department of Education of the Conference, Dowling fought to overturn the bigoted Oregon Law which declared that it was a misdemeanor for any parent to fail to send a child between the ages of 8 and 16 to a public school. The Supreme

Holy Trinity Church and School, New Ulm

Court declared this law unconstitutional in June, 1925. The American hierarchy declared the outcome a triumph for the principle of freedom in education and religion.

Dowling furthered diocesan works of charity. He authorized the Diocesan Bureau of Catholic Charities to be incorporated under the leadership of Rev. J. F. Doherty in 1920. This was an attempt to centralize and coordinate all Catholic charities in St. Paul and

Ramsey County. The Bureau sought to find homes for the adoption of orphans and neglected children and acted as their legal guardian. The Rev. R. W. Doherty became the Bureau's second director, giving able guidance to the operation of the Bureau well into the 1950s. The Catholic Infant Home with its care of unwed mothers, the Catholic Boys' Home in Minneapolis, the Catholic Girls and St. Joseph's Orphanages in St. Paul - all were under the supervision of the Bureau.

Early in his episcopacy, Dowling made known his plan for consolidating the diocesan educational system. Besides having all of Catholic education in the diocese under one supervisor, building plans were necessary. The diocese would erect a Preparatory Seminary for aspirants to the

Immaculate Conception Church, Faribault, 1868

priesthood; it would erect a Normal School for the training of sister teachers of all the religious communities engaged in school work in the diocese; and the diocese would erect high schools at strategic points for the graduates of the parochial schools. There was also a plan whereby the diocese would set up a permanent fund for the upkeep of all of its educational institutions. The vision was there but it would take some years before much of that vision would become a reality.

Nazareth Hall, the Preparatory Seminary, was the apple of Dowling's eye. Planned in 1921, the Hall opened September 12, 1923. The campus flanked the shore of Lake Johanna, outside the corporate limits of the Twin Cities. The land had been purchased by Bishop Grace in 1866 and still belonged to the diocese. Dowling would tolerate no criticism of any kind concerning the minor seminary. He furnished a suite of rooms at Nazareth for his retreats and frequent visits.

The Diocesan Teachers' College became a reality when the daughters of James J. Hill in 1925 presented their father's residence as a gift to the diocese with the condition that it be used as a normal school for the teaching sisters in the diocese. Classes began in 1927 under the direction of Rev. James A. Byrne.

Sisters at the Diocesan Teacher's College, Hill House, 1935

Classes, held on Saturdays and during the summer, offered a curriculum that embraced all the courses given in the best normal schools plus courses in sound theology. The school functioned under the charter of the College of St. Thomas and in the 1950s was incorporated into the teaching program at the College of St. Catherine. Hundreds of sisters, as well as lay women, became certified diocesan teachers in compliance with Minnesota state statutes.

Catholic secondary education was also of great concern to area Catholics. Dowling approved a much needed improved De La Salle High School for boys in Minneapolis. The old school founded by the Christian Brothers in 1900 had become outmoded so the bishop appealed to the parishes of Minneapolis for funds for the project. The new school was dedicated March 11, 1923, although the new residence and chapel for the Christian Brothers was not undertaken until 1951. Catholic secondary education for girls in

Students and Faculty, Nazareth Hall, 1950s

Academy of the Visitation, Saint Paul, 1881

Minneapolis was provided at St. Margaret's Academy and the Academy of the Holy Angels, both of which were operated under the auspices of the Sisters of St. Joseph. St. Paul's Catholic boys could attend Cretin High School, operated by the Christian Brothers, or St. Thomas Academy, staffed by diocesan clergy, on the grounds of St. Thomas College. St. Paul had St. Joseph's Academy and Derham Hall, operated by the Sisters of St. Joseph of Carondelet, and Visitation Convent School, operated by the Visitandines.

In 1925 the Catholic Education Association gave formal approval of St. Thomas and St. Catherine Colleges in St. Paul, St. Mary's and St. Teresa's Colleges in Winona, and St. John's University in Collegeville. The association declared that all standard requirements had been met. It also acted as supervisor of standardization for the high schools in the diocese.

It was at the parochial level that the greatest visible presence of Catholic education made its mark. For the most part this included grades from kindergarten through eighth grade. Here is where the service of women religious serving their church showed the greatest progress for the diocese in education. In 1921 about 24,000 young people were being trained in diocesan parochial schools. The schools were staffed by many religious communities: Sisters of St. Joseph, School Sisters of Notre Dame, Sisters of St. Benedict, Dominican Sisters from Sinsinawa, Sisters of Christian Charity, Franciscan Sisters from Milwaukee, Franciscan Sisters from Toledo, Poor Handmaids of Jesus, Felician Sisters, and Benedictine Sisters from Duluth. These apostolic

Second Building of the Academy of Holy Angels, Minneapolis, 1900

communities saw the need of a vast Catholic immigrant throng and gave tirelessly of their services to parish communities. In addition, these dedicated religious also ran hospitals, orphanages, homes for the aged, retreat centers for women, and provided for the domestic needs of the major and minor seminaries.

The needs of Catholic rural America were also of great concern to Archbishop Dowling. The Rural Life Conference, founded in 1923, held its 3rd Annual Conference in St. Paul in 1925. Speakers from Illinois, Oregon, as well as Minnesota and Iowa addressed the place of the rural parish and its role in the economy of the church. Topics discussed included: religious vacation schools, religious correspondence courses, vocations from rural areas, Catholic racial groups in rural America, and census-taking in country parishes. At the time of the Diamond Jubilee of the diocese in 1925, the *Catholic Bulletin* noted the growth of the Catholic Church beyond the Twin Cities. Churches had been built at Buffalo, Columbia Heights, Sacred Heart, Faribault, Farmington, Litchfield, Maple Lake, Marshall, Montgomery, Mound, Osseo, Prior Lake, Rosemount, and Tracy. Schools had been erected in Clara City, Lamberton, Loretto, Silver Lake, and Wabasso. New Catholic High

Immaculate Conception Church, St. Peter (destroyed by a tornado, 1998)

51

St. Joseph's Church, Red Wing

Schools had been built in New Ulm and Bird Island.

Only feeble attempts at ecumenism were evident at this time of development. At the time of the Diamond Jubilee, Dowling called for a broader spirit of toleration and good will among the citizens of the region in religious, political, commercial, and social life. He appealed to leaders of all religious denominations to fraternize with one another, to emphasize basic principles of Christian conduct, and to cooperate so that all could enjoy political liberty and religious freedom. He called for an end to social ostracism, religious animosity, and economic injustice since the Fatherhood of God and the brotherhood of human beings were fundamental to all people. Yet, when Rev. John A. Ryan of Catholic University authored an

ecumenical prayer with a rabbi and a Protestant minister as an act against the bigotry of the KKK in Indiana, Dowling refused to support the measure.

However, Dowling was forward-looking in supporting the National Catholic Welfare Conference's denunciation of war and economic imperialism that would force whole nations under the dominance of more powerful ones. Struggles over war debts from WWI, reparation payments, trade barriers, and immigration restrictions were of great concern to social activists of the time. Aware of these justice concerns, Dowling spoke eloquently upholding the Catholic social encyclicals of Pope Leo XIII and Pope Pius XI, so championed by Rev. John A. Ryan and other social activists. This was especially true in his defense of unionism and the rights of workers as laid down by Leo XIII and defended in the diocese through the able teaching of Ryan. Dowling's influence could also be seen at the International Conference on the Limitation of Armaments in 1922 during President Harding's administration. His advice to Harding to take practical steps toward decreasing armaments was laudable but proved to be too little and too late to stave off the advance of new European dictators. Dowling also supported the National Catholic Service School for Women, a Washington, D.C. graduate professional school for the training of Catholic social

Basilica of St. Mary, Minneapolis, baldaquin altar

St. Bernard's Church, Saint Paul, 1890

workers under the auspices of the National Council of Catholic Women and under the direction of the Catholic University of America. In conjunction with this, Dowling respected the National Council of Catholic Women as an integral part of the National Catholic Welfare Conference. He lauded its object of bringing Catholic Women's organizations of the state into closer relations for mutual helpfulness and especially for the promotion of higher education. Diocesan Councils were organized, of course, according to the wishes of the bishop. The National Council of Catholic Women undertook the promotion of study clubs, Christian instruction for training instructors in Catholic doctrine for Catholic rural districts and for the weekday religion release classes.

The Mexican Revolution of 1911 with its strong anti-Catholic bent and expulsion of Catholic bishops and priests generated strong responses from the National Catholic Welfare Conference in the United States. A large number of Mexican Catholics found their way into the St. Paul Archdiocese. The N.C.W.C.'s concern over Americanization compelled the local council to make first contact with these immigrants, but it had to work through Archbishop Dowling. Local animosity pushed by the KKK plus agitation for passing the National Quotas Act (limiting immigration) caused special problems for this immigrant group. Mexican immigrants tended to congregate on the flats of the levee in St. Paul. Ultimately they would organize their parish community, Our Lady of Guadalupe. This Mexican Question demanded the attention of the N.C.W.C. because it was thought of as a Catholic rights' question. This group asked the federal government to intervene. The U.S. State Department would do nothing positive to protest Mexico's treatment of its Catholics because Evangelical Protestants and the KKK in the Mid-west were too strong. Dowling even petitioned President Coolidge to protest

Mexico's action but other American bishops advised the N.C.W.C. to be cautious. The bishops' advice was to avert war through negotiation. Dowling was accused of interjecting church affairs into America's foreign policy. The church/state issue over control of education of American youth remained a very hot issue. Anti-Catholicism became a very strong issue in presidential politics from 1914 to 1928 and the local press brought accusations and rebuttals of Catholics being unAmerican to the grass-roots level in the archdiocese. These affairs kept the local and national Church on the defensive.

In the works of mercy supported by Dowling, none can compare with his persistent support of Catholic education. Dowling was an excellent teacher. He often served as the devil's advocate in his attempt to probe all sides of an issue. He was involved in the reorganization of N.C.E.A. (National Catholic Educational Association) in 1919. He supported the Knights of Columbus program to educate ex-servicemen after World War I. He praised their initiatives in gathering monographs of the experiences of various ethnic groups as they migrated to America and became true Americans. By establishing the Archbishop Ireland Fund for Education

Knights of Columbus in procession

in 1920 and raising $2.5 million for Catholic education in the diocese, he called Catholic lay leadership to active participation in the educational arm of the local Church. The people of the diocese rose to the occasion during some hard times. He called laywomen to participate in the venture as they had never participated before. He encouraged women's sodalities in the parishes for the purpose of giving women a base of operation for carrying out charitable works of the church. During his time 20 new parish schools were opened. At the time of his death the archdiocesan system included three high schools for boys, six for girls, 17 parochial high and 113 grade schools with an attendance of 35,000 children.

A weak heart and lungs plagued Dowling during the last years of his life. He died November 29, 1930 with his good friend, Father Walsh (co-founder of Maryknoll) at his side. After a memorial service attended by several American clerical dignitaries, his interment took place at Calvary Cemetery. Dowling left a legacy of building expansion, administrative consolidation, and educational thrust to the archdiocese. He had made a mark on the men of letters of his day for his preaching and writing.

> *"Thus the bishops, by praying and toiling for the people, apportion in many different forms and without stint, that which flows from the abundance of Christ's holiness. By the example and manner of life they should exercise a powerful influence for good on those over whom they are placed."*
>
> *Lumen Gentium*

JOHN GREGORY MURRAY, was a leader in sharp contrast to his predecessor and a man of the people, whose style of pastoral shepherding during the hard times of the Great Depression made its mark on Catholics and non-Catholics alike. His coat of arms bearing his motto, "Mea Omnia Tua" (All that I have is yours) attests to his style of leadership. Born in Waterbury, Connecticut, on February 26, 1877, Murray completed his training for the priesthood in Louvain,

Archbishop John Gregory Murray

Belgium, and was ordained for the diocese of Hartford, Connecticut, on April 11, 1900. In Louvain he had acquired a reputation for exceptionally high scholastic achievement, a manly character, and a generous spirit. These qualities made him remembered as "the good John Murray." He was consecrated Bishop of Hartford April 18, 1920, and in 1925 became Bishop of Portland, Maine. He was awarded an honorary doctorate from Louvain in 1927 on the occasion of the 500th anniversary of the founding of that Catholic university. He was appointed Archbishop of St. Paul on October 29, 1931. Leaving his bishopric of Portland, Maine, he arrived in St. Paul, January 27, 1932.

Murray's first appointments set the tone of continuity that would mark his episcopacy in St. Paul. He appointed The Right Rev. James C. Byrne Vicar General of the diocese, reaffirmed Monsignor Lawrence Ryan as rector of the Cathedral, and reappointed the staff in the Chancery Office. He took up residency at 226 Summit Ave, where he remained for five and a half years. Vacating the residence to provide accommodations for the sisters attending the summer session of the Diocesan

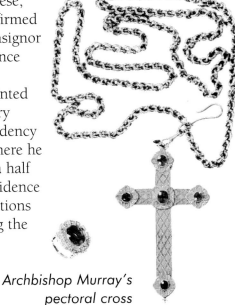
Archbishop Murray's pectoral cross

Teachers College, he moved to quarters in the Cathedral rectory where he lived with the priests of the parish and Chancery Office.

Murray's first Confirmation took place February 23, 1932 in the chapel of St. Margaret's Academy, Minneapolis. There he confirmed a class of deaf mutes who had completed preparations and a retreat at the Basilica of St. Mary. About 125 people attended the ceremony; 75 of whom were hearing impaired. Ten of these were non-Catholics. Archbishop Murray's sermon was signed by Father Gehl. Rev. W. A. Brand of the Basilica staff served as chaplain for the hearing impaired of the Twin Cities. The archbishop ardently supported this ministry.

The training and spiritual welfare of the sisters in the diocese was of special concern to the archbishop. He urged diocesan clergy to provide for the

training of the sisters teaching in their parochial schools, urging them to make arrangements for the sisters to attend the Diocesan Teachers' College to obtain advanced training in all of the subjects that would impact the lives of children under their care. He was meticulous, almost to a fault, that strict regulations laid down for religious under Canon Law were observed. Throughout his episcopacy, the archbishop kept close relations with the various religious communities serving the church in the St. Paul archdiocese. He gave explicit directions to pastors as to the provisions to be made for sisters coming to teach vacation school during the summer months in their parishes.

Murray believed in the use of radio to reach the scattered throngs of faithful under him. On the CBS program "Church of the Air" as well as on WCCO he spoke of the commission given the Church by Christ to teach all

Archbishop Murray's first confirmation of the deaf, St. Margaret's Academy, Minneapolis

nations all things for all times. He explained how the Church must be ready to enter every field of thought and be a patron of all kinds of learning so that Catholicism might reach all classes of people and bring them to their eternal destiny. Faith and reason were the twin torches the Church must use to illumine the minds of all people throughout the globe. Papal authority would guide the teaching arm of the Church until Christ's mandate would be achieved.

During the times of the Great Depression, it was important to the archbishop that he be one with the people he served. And so he was. It was common to see Archbishop Murray riding the trolleys or walking in the downtown area. Everyone was worthy of a friendly greeting: young business men and women scurrying about their daily routines, old folk waiting for public transit, young school girls walking to their schools. Each person was worthy of recognition. Murray did his utmost to implement the appeal of Pope Pius XI, who in an encyclical letter, *Caritas Dei,* of May 3, 1932 called for all Catholics to unite in a crusade of prayer and penance to alleviate the plight of the downtrodden who were caught in the terrible consequences of the economic crisis which encompassed the entire world. Besides ordering a novena of prayer and a special mission in each parish, he organized a crusade of charity in

Meeting of Catholic Rural Life Conference in Saint Paul, 1934

Medal honoring Pope Pius XI

order to solicit contributions for distribution to the needy regardless of creed or color. These contributions were to be used in cooperation with whatever agencies of relief existed within the community, be they the Community Chest, the St. Vincent de Paul Society, or other similar organizations.

Ethnic celebrations in church events continued to mark activities in the diocese. Men and women of German ancestry continued to celebrate the feast of St. Boniface with great ceremony. The annual celebration was under the sponsorship of the German societies of St. Paul. Throngs crowded the Cathedral, sang German hymns, and listened to addresses given by Archbishop Murray in German and in English. Pastors of St. Mathew's and St. Agnes' parishes arranged the affairs. Not to be outdone, the Italians marked

Nursing Students, at St. Mary's Hospital School of Nursing, Minneapolis, 1931

Columbus Day with like festivities. In May, 1932 three area priests received rare honors from King Victor Emmanuel III of Italy in recognition of their services to Italian immigrants to the Twin Cities. The Right Rev. James C. Byrne, Right Rev. H. Moynihan, and the Very Rev. L. F. Ryan were recognized for their outstanding work. The Ancient Order of Hibernians proved to be an Irish stronghold in St. Paul. Members headed the committee for the religious celebration of St. Patrick's Day with a host of activities beginning with a Solemn High Mass celebrated in the St. Paul Cathedral. This group became active in collecting materials for an Irish archive collection which would ultimately be housed at the College of St. Thomas.

Although Murray warned clergy against meddling in political affairs unless political debates raised the question of a religious or moral problem, he reserved to himself the power of granting permission to speak out in these cases. His ordinance of silence on political issues applied to all Catholic societies, parochial, diocesan, and national as well as to any Catholic Church corporation within the archdiocese. The times, however, were marked by the

CATHOLIC LABOR SCHOOLS

Where . . .
Saint Paul
Cathedral School
Opposite Cathedral
Wednesday Nights
November 3rd until Christmas

Minneapolis
St. Stephens School
2123 Clinton Ave. So.
Friday Nights
November 3rd until Christmas

South St. Paul
Holy Trinity Church
755 4th Ave. So.
Thursday Nights
November 3rd until Christmas

What Is Taught . . .
Catholic Social Teaching
Labor Law
Current Labor Problems

Who Is Eligible . . .
All men and women who are members of Labor Unions

This is a free educational program!

Catholic Labor Schools advertisement

politicization of unions which had become the workers' way of standing up for their rights.

Pope Pius XI had affirmed the rights of workers to unionize and Murray, like other prelates tried to implement the teaching of Pius XI in his diocese. In November, 1935, the archbishop opened the Catholic Labor School, the first such school in the nation. It was first held at St. Joseph's parish in Minneapolis, later moved to St. Bridget's, and then to St. Stephen's, a more central location. Attendance was restricted to Catholic men and women who were members of labor unions. Formal classes were offered in Catholic social teaching, economics, parliamentary law and labor law. Because of World War II, classes were suspended from 1942 to 1946, then resumed at St. Stephen's. A new school was established in the Cathedral parish in St. Paul. Father Francis Gilligan of the St. Paul Seminary was director of the schools which were conducted quietly to avoid large public demonstrations. Priests involved with the schools became well acquainted with labor leaders and were frequently called on as arbitrators in industrial disputes in the region.

Sunday school class, Centerville

The College of St. Thomas had been run by the Holy Cross Fathers from 1928 to 1933. New buildings had increased the indebtedness of the college. Archbishop Murray wanted this indebtedness addressed, so he decided it was imperative to restore the college to diocesan control and assume the indebtedness. After consultation, he asked the Holy Cross Fathers to leave and appointed the Rev. James H. Moynihan to the presidency of the institution. Under constitutional changes, the college again became a diocesan institution. Through the largesse of the priests of the diocese and a very successful alumni campaign, the entire debt was liquidated by 1935.

In order to promote catechetical instruction throughout the diocese, Murray organized the Confraternity of Christian Doctrine in April, 1935. Under the direction of the Rev. R. G. Bandas, the confraternity was to form study clubs in order to advance the religious education of adults and to train teachers for teaching Catholic youth attending public schools during the release periods which were permitted by Minnesota state law. Confraternity summer schools for teachers' training were held at St. Thomas College in St. Paul and at St. Margaret's Academy in Minneapolis. The cultural activity of the Confraternity for the benefit of young men and women of more mature years assumed the form of a Catholic Choral Club under the direction of Rev. F. A. Missia of the St. Paul Seminary. The establishment of the Catholic Youth Centers in St. Paul and Minneapolis also resulted from Confraternity planning and oversight.

Catholic Boy Scouts of America, Basilica of St. Mary, Minneapolis

Ever interested in Catholic youth, Murray established the Catholic Scouting Committee in 1936 for the purpose of awarding worthy scouts meeting the requirements for good scouting. The Committee also initiated the Ad Altare Dei award. This consisted of a bronze cross suspended from a ribbon in papal and national colors. This was given to scouts who served at the altar in any capacity, who knew their religion and the proper Latin responses for the Mass, and who were punctual in observing proper decorum. These awards were presented by the bishop at an annual religious ceremony

The depression years of the 1930s prompted debates over serious social issues. Socialism, communism, anarchy, eugenics, birth control and sterilization were hot issues. A letter of Archbishop Murray dated August 6, 1935, condemned birth control and sterilization and forbade Catholics to accept or retain membership in a society supporting these two evils. He said that people so doing should be denied the sacraments. This image of defensiveness and apologetics was sensed by non-Catholic leaders in Murray's forbidding Catholic youth to participate in glee clubs, school choirs, and similar

Holy Name Society, St. Vincent's Church, Saint Paul, 1922

organizations that participated in programs of worship sponsored by non-Catholic churches. Catholics were forbidden to sing or act in any program designed to support non-Catholic religious activities. This stance cooled the opportunity for ecumenical cooperation throughout the geographic area.

Holy Name Banner, St. Vincent's

Murray was also concerned about the appropriateness of celebrating the liturgy, that it be in compliance with the Motu Proprio of Pius X on church music. He ordered all the churches of the diocese to celebrate each Sunday a Solemn Mass or Missa Cantata with music approved by the Archdiocesan Committee of Sacred Music. The approved text was the *Liber Usualis* and it was unlawful to sing anything in the vernacular at liturgical services of any kind. The organ had to be played according to the regulations of sacred music. The penchant for conformity and unanimity marked the hierarchical model of the church's leadership in America up to the time of the Second Vatican Council. Under the patronage of Archbishop Murray, the St. Paul Diocese hosted the Second National Liturgical Week in St. Paul, Oct. 6-10, 1941. Rev. William Busch of the St. Paul Seminary, an ardent advocate of liturgical reform, was in charge of arrangements. This function brought to St. Paul members of the hierarchy, priests, religious, and laity from all parts of the country who were interested in liturgical reform. This had a profound impact on the mode of liturgical celebration throughout the archdiocese. St. John's Abbey in Collegeville, Minnesota, under the liturgical work of Virgil Michel, O.S.B. had already become known for advancing liturgical reform.

Visit of Cardinal Pacelli (Later Pope Pius XII) to the Archdiocese

In October, 1936 His Eminence Cardinal Pacelli (later Pope Pius XII) arrived in St. Paul while on an unofficial visit to America. After celebrating Mass at the Cathedral and bestowing the Apostolic Blessing on the throngs attending, the cardinal continued his quick visits to 18 different states. In St. Paul he expressed amazement with the flourishing parochial life of the church in this diocese, the social influences, school system, and generosity of the faithful, the frequent, even daily, communion of the faithful, and the close cooperation of clergy and laity in all areas of religious practice.

Despite this image, when the National Conference of Catholic Charities met in St. Paul in August, 1937, hosting some 900 delegates from across the country, attendance was comprised mostly of hierarchy, clergy, and religious. The Superior Council of the St. Vincent de Paul Society and the Conference of Religious met concurrently. Problems concerning families and children's health, youth activities, and social and economic concerns of the times were

addressed. There was one public meeting at which Bishop Muench of Fargo spoke. He was known for his works for social change. The laity seemed far from the core of decision-making for the archdiocese. This was a sign of the times of the pre-Vatican II church throughout the world.

Perhaps the most memorable event of Archbishop Murray's episcopate was the celebration of the Ninth National Eucharistic Congress held in the Twin Cities, June 22-26, 1941. The majority of the American hierarchy, prelates from Canada and Mexico, hundreds of clergy and religious, and tens of thousands of the laity from all parts of the country, especially from the Northwest,

participated. Under the chairmanship of Msgr. James M. Reardon, pastor of the Basilica of St. Mary, Minneapolis, some 22 committees of priests, sisters, lay men, and lay women planned and supervised the celebration.

Ninth Eucharistic Congress advertisement

Ninth National Eucharistic Congress, Saint Paul and Minneapolis, 1941

The Archdiocese of Saint Paul deems it a high honor to offer hospitality to the thousands of pilgrims who assemble from far and near before the throne of our Eucharistic King to pay them a tribute of love, adoration, thanksgiving and reparation while petitioning Him to bestow His mercy on the millions who acknowledge His social sovereignty.

+ John Gregory Murray
Archbishop of Saint Paul

Archbishop John G. Murray convenes the Eucharistic Congress in Saint Paul, 1941

Sacrament from the church of St. Andrew to the Repository in Como Park, thence to the Eucharistic Center at the Minnesota State Fair Grounds for the final ceremony. There the Papal Legate gave the final benediction to the kneeling throng (more than 100,000) despite a downpour of rain. An outgrowth of the Congress was promotion of adoration and devotion to the Blessed Sacrament. Daily exposition of the Blessed Sacrament was initiated at St. Mary's Basilica, St. Lawrence and St. Vincent Churches, and at the chapels of religious sisters in the archdiocese.

Rev. F. A. Missia, Professor of Plain Chant at the St. Paul Seminary, trained adult and children's choirs in the liturgical music used for all events connected with the celebration. His Eminence Dennis Cardinal Dougherty, Archbishop of Philadelphia, was the legate of Pope Pius XII. The general theme of the Congress was "Our Eucharistic Lord Glorified by Sacrifice." The culminating feature of the Congress was a liturgical procession with the Blessed

America's involvement in World War II taxed the human and material resources of the diocese. Men and women went off to the armed services, many never to return. Women answered the need for workers in defense plants in Rosemount, New Brighton, and the manufacturing jobs vacated by men now in the war fields. There was a demand for chaplains; each diocese in the nation was asked to

Tissot monstrance used at the Eucharistic Congress which was brought from France in 1865 by Reverend Felix Tissot, early pastor of St. Anthony Parish

Tissot cruets, 1860s

release up to 10 percent of its priests for service. Over 50 from the archdiocese were accepted, most serving overseas. Although three were seriously wounded in the conflict, they recovered. The shortage of priests on the home front added burdens to the priests remaining. Authorization to officiate at three Masses on Sunday was given to one priest in every parish from which a chaplain was taken. The archbishop called for all parishes to hold prayer vigils and other special services in united appeal for the termination of the war and the safe return of our military personnel.

Because of the government's plan to martial manufacturing and food management to support the nation's war effort, many suffered from shortages in food and clothing. Rationing in all areas of necessity and luxury became the way of life all during the war. With so many men away at war and women working out of the home at all hours of the day, family life suffered strains and dislocations during these years. These needs prompted the establishment of the Diocesan Bureau of Charities in 1943. This was incorporated as a child-placing and family agency under the direction of Rev. Francis W. Curtin with offices in the chancery building in St. Paul. This agency secured foster homes for orphans, homeless, delinquent or children with special needs as well as those surrounded by immoral influences.

Murray's concern over the plight of family life prompted the formation of the Family Guild in 1946 under the spiritual direction of Rev. R. T. Doherty. Its purpose was to work for the restoration of Christian family life, threatened by the secularism of the time. Married couples met in small groups once a month to discuss family problems and seek support in trying to model home life

Church of St. Agnes, Saint Paul

after the example of the Holy Family at Nazareth. This cell movement grew into a federation whose monthly meetings became known as "Cana Days."

Murray endeared himself to the people of his archdiocese by his mingling of his personal acts of charity and prayerful and austere spirituality with his daily duties as bishop during the trying times of the war. As pastor of his bishopric, he deemed it his place to be among the

Interior of Nativity Church

St. Paul Seminary Chapel

During this same time, the St. Paul Seminary achieved secure status on several grounds. It was accredited by the North Central Association and the Dept. of Education of the State of Minnesota. On April 1, 1947, the Accrediting Board of the University of Minnesota declared that it would honor the MA degree granted by the Seminary. The Board of Trustees of the Seminary authorized the adoption of both the BA and the MA programs.

people he served. When he called for special prayer vigils and more austere mortification for the church's appeal for peace, the congregation of the faithful not only listened but followed his example. He provided a stability that the changing times had shattered. When the war finally ceased, returning throngs of weary service men and women accelerated the changes imposed on the post war society throughout the diocese, both in urban and rural areas. Government supported education for returning veterans brought about a large influx of new students to the Twin Cities and other college towns. Government housing sprang up overnight and the development of suburbia began to change living patterns for a society yearning to enjoy the fruits of affluent America. In 1946, 72 temporary housing units on the grounds of St. Thomas attested to the burgeoning of enrollment at that diocesan college. New buildings were projected. By 1950 Albertus Magnus Science building, O'Shaughnessy Hall, and the new Library were erected. In 1947 the college enrollment reached 2,103, including Catholics, Protestant, and Jews. Day students outnumbered boarders four to one.

Appeals of ethnic parishes for church aid to foster the preservation of their respective cultures resulted in the Oblate Sisters of Providence of Baltimore coming to St. Paul on September 30, 1945. They served the Black Catholics of St. Paul through catechetical work and opening a new parochial school in St. Peter Claver parish. The Rev. J. J. Luger was pastor at the time. He had been known for his work dispelling the prejudice and ignorance concerning blacks in the region.

The growth of six diocesan parishes and the work of their pastors who had served as diocesan consulters prompted Archbishop Murray to make these pastors Domestic Prelates. This distinction entitled them to wear the

Interior of St. Paul Seminary Chapel, 1950s

*St. Francis
de Salles Church,
Saint Paul*

royal purple and be addressed as Right
Rev. Monsignor. These pastors who
made such a mark on diocesan affairs
during the 1940s and 1950s were:

Right Rev. John Dunphy of
Ascension Parish
Right Rev. Joseph A. Corrigan of
St. Mark's, St. Paul
Right Rev. Aloysius Ziskovsky of
St. Matthew's, St. Paul
Right Rev. James Zachman of St.
Francis de Sales, St. Paul
Right Rev. John J. Cullinan of St.
Luke's, St. Paul
Right Rev. Vincent W.Worzalla of
Holy Cross, Minneapolis.

Despite the losses during the war, the
Catholic Church in the upper Mid-west
enjoyed expansion. The Catholic
population in the archdiocese in 1945
reached 294, 861 while the entire state
of Minnesota claimed 526, 785
Catholics. In 1945 the Most Rev. Francis
J. Schenk, rector of the Cathedral and
Vicar General of the diocese, was
consecrated Bishop of Crookston,
Minnesota. In 1947, Bishop James J.
Byrne was consecrated auxiliary to
Archbishop Murray in St. Paul. Bishop
Byrne assumed many functions of the
local ordinary as Archbishop Murray's
health became seriously taxed.

The year 1949 marked the 100th
Minnesota Territorial Anniversary with
October 9th designated as Centennial
Sunday. All Minnesota dioceses held
special prayer services and spiritual
events to commemorate the occasion.
The following year, the solemn
commemoration of the 100th
anniversary of the Diocese of St. Paul
was the most significant religious event
of 1950. The culminating activities took
place in the Twin Cities during the week
of October 15. The Most Rev. T. A.

*Crucifixion Scene,
Holy Cross
Church*

Welch of Duluth presided at the
celebration of a Pontifical Mass in the St.
Paul Auditorium. The Proper of the
Mass was sung by the seminarian choir
of nearly 300 voices and the Common of
the Mass by 6,000 young people from
Catholic parish and high schools of the
diocese. The liturgical music was under
the direction of the Rev. A. Missia. The
archdiocese also sponsored a civic
meeting where several thousand
assembled to listen to a program
of classical and modern music
sung by the St. Paul Catholic
Choral Society, also under
the direction of Rev.
Missia. The final event
of the anniversary
celebration was a
pontifical high Mass
offered by Archbishop
Murray in the
Seminary Chapel
which focused on the
work and study of the
bishops, priests, and
seminarians of the
diocese. Woven into this
celebration was the
conferring of the MA

*Statue from
Ascension Church,
Minneapolis*

degree on five priests ordained that year. This was a first in the history of the seminary and did much to enhance the prestige of the St. Paul Seminary in its priestly training and curriculum offerings.

As part of the centennial of the diocese the archbishop initiated an educational expansion program. Two sites for high schools for boys were purchased, one in St. Paul and one in Minneapolis. A parish grade school was to be transferred to a teaching community of sisters, the Sisters of the Blessed Virgin Mary (B.V.M.s), who were to open it in 1951 as a High School for girls. Parishes were asked to participate in these plans for new inter-parish high schools. During the 1950s the number of parochial elementary schools increased from 128 to 146. Enrollment increased from 33,089 to 45,812. Parish high schools increased from 16 to 19, with enrollment increasing from 1551 to 4008. St. Thomas College served 1624 students; the College of St. Catherine listed 955 students. The Catholic population in the

Bishop Leonard Cowley greeting officers of the National Council of Catholic Women

archdiocese grew to almost 369,660 by the end of the decade. This spurt of growth was primarily in urban areas while rural areas noted a decline in population.

The personal charity of Archbishop Murray inspired actions of charity sponsored by the diocese. Mission Sunday collections provided aid not only for home missions and the Society for the Propagation of the Faith, but also for relief through the Catholic Near East Welfare Association which was under the presidency of the Cardinal Archbishop of New York. Under Murray, the archdiocese also contributed to the Central European Rehabilitation Association which aimed to help the destitute of Central Europe after WWII. Local committees that collected medical and food supplies, clothing, books, and cash for fuel and housing needs, were organized in various communities with the major office in Minneapolis. The diocese also participated in the Christian Rural Overseas Program which was established jointly by Catholics, Protestants, and Lutherans, with central offices in Chicago. This program provided food trains for overseas relief through local churches. Catholic Rural Life was a major sponsor of this program.

Under Murray's supervision, women in the diocese continued their charitable works through many organizations. As early as 1933 he helped organize the St. Paul Archdiocesan Council of Catholic Women, later called the Guild of Catholic Women. This was a federation of women's organizations, parochial and non parochial, which aimed to promote apostolic activities in response to the papal call for programs of Catholic Action. This group played an important part in promoting the program of the

Confraternity of Christian Doctrine. The Guild became involved in Red Cross work, youth and adult education, distribution of Catholic literature, care of the sick, infirm, aged, and underprivileged, family life, home and school issues, youth problems, lay retreats, foreign missions, scholarship funds, radio and television, and rural

Church of the Sacred Heart, Saint Paul

or sterilization. His decree was read in all Catholic churches within the archdiocese since it affected physicians, nurses, social workers in a special way as well as affecting all laity. This stance brought vilifying mail from those within and outside the Catholic Church who disagreed with him. Margaret Sanger criticized

life issues. Catholic women were urged to take an active part in community, national, and inter-national affairs and to be well-informed, articulate Catholic women. During the 1940s the Guild fought to be allowed to represent Catholic girls appearing in juvenile court. Women also participated in the Legion of Mary work, the Daughters of Isabella who followed the Knights of Columbus programs, and the Catholic Daughters of America who raised money for the education of priests and the operating of vacation schools for Catholic children in rural communities.

The energies of the archbishop were in demand from many areas of need among his congregation. He approved the Twin City De L'Epee Club of the deaf and appointed the pastor of the deaf as moderator of the club. Attempting to address the chemical dependency problem among his clergy, he authorized the Hazelden Foundation to accept clergy of the diocese for treatment. He spoke out vociferously against birth control and ordered all Catholics to renounce membership and employment in organizations advocating birth control

the archbishop for his stand on birth control in angry and condemnatory articles in national magazines. Within his diocese, Murray won strong support from the Catholic Aid Association, a German-Catholic benevolent society, and the Catholic Women's Union of the Central Verein which also set up programs to assist prospective mothers in defraying the cost of confinement and in promoting respect for the Catholic ideals of marriage and motherhood.

Archbishop Murray was seriously ill when his 50th anniversary of ordination approached. He refused any public celebration. All he would agree to was a Pontifical Mass in the Cathedral which was filled beyond capacity. Knowing that the clergy and others wanted to do more to celebrate and show their love for their archbishop, the consulters for planning the jubilee celebration finally convinced the archbishop to allow special contributions to defray costs. Some of these funds helped pay for outstanding obligations covering charity demands which the archbishop had personally addressed and for which no diocesan funds were available.

As the archbishop aged and cancer drained his energies, he still struggled to meet the obligations of his office. His fierce and meticulous sense of duty attached to his high church office remained a driving force for him until his death in October, 1956. People of all faiths mourned the loss of a stalwart and beloved pastor. Steady streams of mourners filed past the casket and attended the final services in the Cathedral. Archbishop Murray was the first of the St. Paul Diocese's archbishops to be interred in Resurrection Cemetery in Mendota.

Archbishop William O. Brady

Pastor of St. Agnes Parish in St. Paul appointed first bishop. Rev. Schladweiler and Rev. Leonard Cowley were consecrated bishops at the same time in the St. Paul Cathedral by Archbishop Brady. Cowley became an auxiliary to Brady. Brady undertook immediate action planning a new bishop's residence and chancery office building on property directly across from the Cathedral. Until these facilities were completed, Brady resided in the chaplain's quarters at the College of St. Catherine where his sister, Mary William Brady, C.S.J. was president.

Archbishop Brady's medals and ring

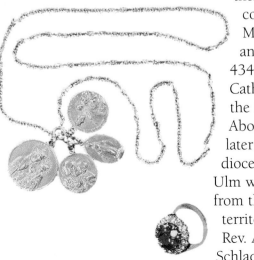

WILLIAM O. BRADY succeeded to the office of Archbishop of St. Paul on Oct. 11, 1956. His jurisdiction extended then over 27 counties in Minnesota and over 434,000 Catholics in the region. About a year later the diocese of New Ulm was carved from that territory with Rev. Alphonse Schladweiler,

Born at Fall River, Massachusetts, Feb. 1. 1899, Brady entered St. Mary's Seminary in Baltimore in 1918, completing an MA in philosophy in 1920. Receiving an MA from the Sulpician Seminary in Washington, D.C., in 1923, he was ordained in Fall Rivers Dec. 23, 1923. Together with Rev. James L. Connolly, and Rev. Francis Gilligan, Brady accepted the invitation of Archbishop Dowling to come to St. Paul and became incardinated in the Archdiocese of St. Paul. In 1925 Brady received the degree of Licentiate of Sacred Theology (S.T. L) from the Angelicum Pontifical College in Rome. He entered a lifetime of teaching, first as a seminary professor and rector

68

Archbishop Brady and Confirmation class, Hugo

in St. Paul, next as Bishop of Sioux Falls, South Dakota, and from 1956 until his death in 1962 as Archbishop of St. Paul. Archbishop Murray appointed him rector of the St. Paul Seminary in 1933. Appointed by Pope Pius XII as Bishop of Sioux Falls, he was consecrated bishop in 1939. In 1956 he became coadjutor archbishop of St. Paul with the right of succession.

Archbishop Brady coupled his vision for a strong and vibrant church in his diocese with the energy of a doer and forward-looking decision-maker. He provided a chaplain for the Catholic boys at the correctional school in Red Wing and provided funds for upgrading the chapel facility at the institution. He relaxed the Eucharistic fast for the inmates in order to accommodate for the meal schedule of the facility. The Catholic chaplain was to cooperate with chaplains from other faiths in the use of the chapel facility. Under Brady's directives, various Catholic charity groups in the diocese acted in collaboration with the Community Chest of St. Paul, The Very Rev. George E. Ryan, Rector of the Cathedral and a member of

the Board of Directors of the Community Chest, coordinated cooperative ventures. When freeway construction threatened to dissect parish communities, displacing many families of the working class in the region, Brady requested the Housing and Redevelopment Authority to seek advice from the various pastors who would be involved.

The Cold War was still a national crisis that involved Americans even at the local level. Fear of retaliation against the United States by the U.S.S.R., now capable of using atomic power, prompted a National Civil Defense Program with all sorts of specifications should an atomic attack take place. Parish priests were asked to participate actively in Civil Defense procedures. The Minnesota State Religious Affairs Service became an arm of National Civil Defense. The archdiocese was an active participant. In a war emergency, the normal functions of the clergy and churches were to be expanded and intensified to provide spiritual help to distressed people.

Prudence mosaic, Cathedral

This period marked the birth of the baby boomers, suburbia, affluent America and the debate over birth control became more strident. New drugs appeared on the market, creating a major debate over the advisability of their use. Brady sought the advice of local doctors, since it was imperative that Catholic priests be informed on the effects of these drugs on contraception. Brady was assured by reputable doctors that the drugs were good, but how they were used was the problem. The moral issue of the sacredness of life remained the central issue.

Another growing health awareness focused on mental illness. When asked to authorize a program for Clergymen's Orientation to Mental Health at the Hastings State Hospital, Brady reluctantly approved the dissemination of the data announcing the course, but he still advised that the program be urged on laymen. Sister Annette Walters, C.S.J., Ph.D., served on the Board of Directors of the Minnesota Association for Mental Health and worked hard to get priests to attend the workshop, as she considered churches and synagogues key elements in the program. Sister's work with religious

Baldaquin and dome interior of Cathedral

Church of St. Joseph, Hopkins

and priests in the area of mental health was of great service to the entire church community.

Archbishop Brady did much to further the completion of interior decoration of the Cathedral. In the early 1950s Right Rev. George Ryan had initiated work on the interior of the dome and its supporting pillars. The high windows in the dome and transepts,, mosaics depicting the Cardinal Virtues, and statues of the four evangelists were completed in time for the formal consecration of the St. Paul Cathedral October 14, 1958 by the archbishop. The hard times of the Depression Years were past and the more affluent times made it feasible to resume plans for completing the interior Cathedral decoration. and consecration. The archbishop wanted a special Rosary Crusade as part of Father Peyton's national crusade to be in conjunction with the consecration of the Cathedral. The plan was to collaborate with the other dioceses in Minnesota in a joint pastoral on the Rosary Crusade. The event was indeed a gala celebration. Affluent times also gave rise to philanthropic groups wishing to generate funds to better the Republic. The Ford Foundation, one of these, tried to excite organizations to consider problems and

Church of St. Casmir, Saint Paul

and effectiveness that Catholic principles could bring to a society sorely in need of them. Brady called for a positive press to abandon an apologetic defensiveness and rather to challenge its readers to a more active living of the Gospel message. He strove to use the diocesan newspaper, *The Catholic Bulletin,* as a tool to try to make it *God's Home Journal* in the archdiocese. His weekly column in that paper attested to his style of leadership with its future vision for the church in America. *The Catholic Digest,* published in St. Paul under the presidency of Rev. Louis A. Gales, had a circulation of about 900,000 in 1958, with subscribers in Germany, Holland, Ireland, England, and Italy. At the time, the Catechetical Guild under the leadership of Rev. Paul Bussard developed a leaflet missal as a substitute for the 14 million or so ordinary parish bulletins used in the archdiocese at that time.

to address needs that most had been avoiding. When Catholic schools applied for some of these funds to help defray the costs of new programs, opposition arose. Major opposition focused on the use of public school buses to transport parochial school children. Opponents queried "When public bus service is provided for parochial school children, is this interference with the separation of church and state?" The Catholic leadership response was "Or is it a practical recognition of the contribution of the church in providing schools that the community otherwise could not afford?" The old controversy had not died.

An area wherein Archbishop Brady shone and posed a marked change from his predecessors in the St. Paul Archdiocese was his leadership in revising the diocesan newspaper. He noted that the weakness of the diocesan press seemed to be that it merely recorded what Catholics had done and gave little attention to challenge the faithful to address what they might be doing better. He called on the Catholic press to supply the leadership

The episcopacy of Archbishop Brady injected a great deal of common sense into prescribed rituals for the reception of the Sacraments. He supported shortening the rite of bringing Holy Communion to the sick. He fully utilized the discretionary powers delegated

Statue from St. Anne's Church, Minneapolis

71

to the bishops by the Sacred Congregation of Rites. He used his judgment how best to authorize his local Church to address the prescribed rituals of the Church. It was more important to follow the spirit of the law rather its letter. Brady wanted the Church in his diocese to be relevant to the changing times and the changing needs of the people his Church was there to serve.

Archbishop Brady challenged Catholics in his archdiocese to active service in the church. He furthered the work of women's groups and acknowledged their contributions: The Archdiocesan Council of Catholic Women, Catholic Daughters of America, Daughters of Isabella, the League of Catholic Women, and the regional chapter of the National Council of

Stained glass window, Annunciation Church, Minneapolis

St. Helena Church, Minneapolis

Catholic Women. He promoted the extension of Lay Volunteers for the Home Missions and Papal Volunteers for Latin America. Because of his premature death, he was never able to realize plans for other lay volunteer programs he envisioned for the archdiocese. Brady's support of the Calix Society for alcoholic priests had positive ramifications throughout the country. He also supported organizing St. Pius X House, a rooming house for young Catholic workers. This was a project of the Young Christian Workers, which planned Catholic mixers and other activities for Catholic youth 25 years of age and under. Cells of YCW were organized in several parishes: St. Thomas and St. Cyril in Minneapolis; Cathedral, St. Rose of Lima, St. Michael, and St. Francis in St. Paul. The YCW was primarily a social movement using specialized techniques for training young adult leaders. The movement aimed to help modern youth discover a spirit of Christian charity, responsibility, and service that would enable them to help establish a more Christian social, political, and parish order. Special courses were provided that aimed to encourage these young people to become dedicated lay apostles in the Church.

Archbishop Brady was truly a realist concerning the place of the Catholic church in America. He saw the challenge the church of his day had to face in fighting to make sound principles in public life prevail. Only then, he said, would the United States remain dominant over communism, fascism, secularism or any other "ism" that might arise. The church, of necessity, had to work within the society in which it existed, addressing the changes that society imposed on all.

While a teacher and later a rector of the St. Paul Seminary, Brady was renowned as a supreme liturgist. For him there was no joy without union with God and the means of attaining that union was Christian liturgical worship. Brady was in Rome when Pius XII approved the new ritual of Holy Week. Immediately he extended to all ordinaries of the archiepiscopal province a general permission for the celebration of the Easter Vigil at whatever time would be locally advantageous.

During the 1950s the bishops of the United States agreed that it was time to call for the optional use of English in connection particularly with Baptism, Marriage, the Sacrament of the Sick, and burial services. Brady was a member of a special Liturgical Committee charged to draw up a manuscript calling for this change. The United States bishops approved the document, but misunderstanding in Rome over some of the specifics delayed action on the United States bishops' request. A great deal of confusion ensued until finally put to rest

when Vatican Council II approved the use of the vernacular in liturgical rites.

Recognized as a leader in the hierarchy of the American church, Brady was made assistant chairman of the Department of Social Action of the N.C.W.C. He became treasurer of the administrative board in 1958 and was reelected twice to that position. In 1958 he was also elected vice chairman of the Episcopal Committee for the Liturgical Apostolate. Bishops Albert Meyer of Chicago and Leo Dworschak of Fargo served with him to produce the document *Collectio Rituum* which updated sacramental and liturgical rituals, leaving much to the discretion of the local ordinary. These bishops were very conscious of the need for reform that Pope John XXIII was advising in announcing the Second Vatican Council.

During a flight to Rome while working on a pre-conciliar commission preparing for the convening of the Second Vatican council, Archbishop Brady suffered a coronary thrombosis and died in Rome October 1, 1961. The hospital chaplain and his sister, Sister Mary William, C.S.J. were with him at the end.

During his short reign in the diocese, Archbishop Brady had begun many

Archbishop Brady meets with Pope John XXIII in Rome prior to the Second Vatican Council

Pope John XXIII

projects that would be completed by his successor. During his tenure, four new parishes were created and a $10 million high school expansion program was inaugurated. Four new high schools had been built and plans for seven more were in the formative stage. He had established the "Opus Sancti Petri" program to further vocations to the priesthood and religious life. His plan, officially approved by Pope John XXIII, recruited 20,000 workers who canvassed the diocese seeking prayers and material help for the education of young men to the priesthood. The response of the laity to the program was phenomenal.

The untimely death of Archbishop Brady was a great loss, not merely to the Archdiocese of St. Paul, but also to the Church in the United States. He was recognized as one of America's great religious leaders. Clergy and laity of the diocese had responded to his leadership. They singled him out as a a spiritual father and as a champion of the Church. His brilliant vision, love for the church, and persuasive teaching prepared his flock for the challenges and changes that the Second Vatican Council would provide.

That Council was indeed a watershed for the Catholic Church in the United States. The apologetic and rigid organizational structures of the tridentine church had to make accommodations for the leadership that would be shared by all of the people of God - pope, bishops, clergy, religious, laity - awakened to the truth that each person had responsibility for making the Church of Christ a living reality in modern times. The individualism of the modern age had to be addressed by focusing on the personhood of each individual with all of the responsibility that such dignity demanded. A church defined as the "People of God" could no longer thrive with narrow and limiting definitions and proscriptions.

The immigrant church of the United States, a refuge and support for so many newcomers to America throughout the 19th century, was no longer meaningful for those prepared for change that challenged them to a more active, authentic, and integral part of the Church in fulfilling all that Christ demanded of His followers.

Pope Paul VI

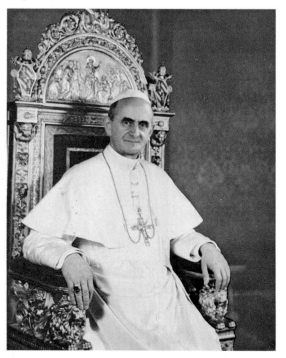

"*That all humankind may be led into the unity of the family of God.*"

Gaudium et Spes

The most earth-shaking event of the 20th century impacting the life of the Catholic Church in the Archdiocese of St. Paul and Minneapolis, indeed in the entire world, was the Second Vatican Council. After almost four years of preparation, the Council opened in Rome on October 11, 1962 under the pontificate of Pope John XXIII and was concluded in 1965 under the pontificate of Pope Paul VI. Archbishop William Brady had been very active in preparatory work for the Council. At the final session of Vatican II, attended by Archbishop Binz and Auxiliary Bishops Cowley, O'Keefe and Shannon of the archdiocese, the Bishops completed and promulgated several documents which they had discussed and debated during the earlier sessions. The document, *Lumen Gentium,* was a breakthrough of the structures that had defined Church for so many over such a long period of time. The Church was now seen as the People of God, emphasizing the inclusive thrust of the

Bishops of the Archdiocesan Province in Rome for the Second Vatican Council

Gospel message. The final document, *The Pastoral Constitution on the Church in the Modern World,* was promulgated by Pope Paul VI on December 7, 1965 and addressed the complex issues faced by the People of God in a rapidly changing world. This lengthy document attests to the conviction of the Council Fathers that the Church was indeed very relevant to a modern and evolutionary society. With the plan of hope for Church reform heralded to the entire world, it fell to the leadership of the local Church to implement plans called for in the documents.

Under the educated leadership of Archbishop Brady, who served on a planning commission for Vatican II, the faithful of the archdiocese had developed high expectations for what the Council would mean in their lives as gospel people. Priests of the archdiocese had worked since the late 1950s in preparation for the anticipated changes. When the Council decrees were published, most priests were ready for their implementation. For many of the laity the council documents called them to more active participation in fulfilling Christ's mandate to go forth and teach all nations by sharing some of the authority heretofore deemed only the jurisdiction of bishops and clergy. The Church in America was no longer an immigrant Church. Nor would the hierarchical, triumphal image of Church satisfy the faithful. The bishop's role was seen as pastor of the local diocesan Church in collaboration with the priests and laity in carrying the gospel message into all walks of life. The laity looked for more visible roles in church affairs. Women and the marginalized in society had high expectations of greater inclusion in Church life. St. Paul's archbishop reminded the faithful that the council was necessary to make all conscious of the unity and universality of the Church and aware of personal concern with the Church in every corner of the world. As shepherd, the archbishop would take his place among the people of God as "servant."

Nevertheless, this sharing in priestly authority in no way diminished the leadership role of those in the episcopal hierarchy. The power of the bishops over the individual Churches entrusted to them called for greater delegation and coordination of that priestly mission. Increased diversity within local parishes and the dioceses generally demanded new approaches to effect consensus on hosts of problems demanding attention. Terms from the Vatican II documents like collegiality, mutuality, and subsidiarity colored discussions about new insights into the Church in the modern world augmented by the Council fathers. Priests, religious, and laity were anxious to make these terms a reality in their lives as the People of God.

Angel from the Cathedral of Saint Paul

> *"Ours is a new age of history with critical and swift upheavals spreading gradually to all corners of the earth."*
>
> Gaudium et Spes

LEO BINZ assumed leadership of the St. Paul and Minneapolis Archdiocese in 1962. The Civil Rights Movement and the Vietnam War prompted social action protests during this time among secular and religious groups throughout America. This affected many groups within the archdiocese. Vatican II had called for personal responsibility in all areas of life. Yet, how would this mandate merge with the notion of separation of Church and state, so embedded in the psyche of American culture? Providing leadership in this regard proved no easy task for the archbishop of St. Paul.

Archbishop Leo Binz

University in Rome. Ordained in Rome March 15, 1924, Binz had served as an instructor at the North American College and then as pastor in various churches in Illinois , and as a staff member of the Apostolic Delegate in Washington. He served as bishop of Winona, Minnesota, and as Archbishop of Dubuque, Iowa, before becoming Archbishop of St. Paul in 1962. As a new appointee to that diocese, he attended the sessions of the Second Vatican Council and was challenged to implement the documents calling for some radical changes for the people of God.

The most immediate changes Archbishop Binz faced after Vatican II involved those

Archbishop Leo Binz, born in Stockton, Illinois in 1900, had studied at Loras College, St. Mary's Seminary in Baltimore, the Sulpician Seminary in Washington, D.C., the North American College and Gregorian

Archbishop Binz's pectoral cross

Receiving Communion in the hand

pertaining to the liturgy. The work of the Benedictines in Collegeville spearheaded their English edition of the Roman Breviary readily adopted throughout the archdiocese. The work of Augustin Cardinal Bea, President of the Secretariat for Promoting Christian Unity, along with the cooperation of the United Bible Societies eventually produced vernacular Scriptures in a movement that benefited the entire Church. Cardinal Bea had sent questionnaires to all Episcopal Conferences throughout the world as part of their collaborative effort in producing the new translations. The archdiocese was actively involved in this process. The change of the texts and chants of the Mass and the Breviary from Latin to English pleased the majority of Catholics in the diocese, but a vocal minority pleaded for permitting the use of the old Latin Tridentine Mass in the Archdiocese. Permission to say Mass in private homes rested with the

pastor of the proper parish in the late 1960s. In August, 1967 permission to have attendance at Saturday evening Masses fulfill the Sunday obligation was granted. This was prompted by a shortage of priests, increased tourism in the region, and the demands of necessary service occupations. Debates ensued over the reception of Communion in the hand, under both species, more than once a day, and even whether or not the mentally retarded ought to be allowed to receive Holy Communion. Some voiced concern that excesses were taking place in religious services wherein Catholics and non-Catholics participated. Binz's stance was to withhold any formal approbation until Rome had spoken to the issue or until guidelines were presented by the National Council of Catholic Bishops. Norms for the implementation of certain decrees of Vatican II were promulgated in Motu Proprio Ecclesiae Sanctae, released by Rome August 12, 1966.

St. John's Abbey Church, Collegeville, 1990

> *"The Church is interested in one thing only to carry on the work of Christ under the guidance of the Holy Spirit."*
>
> *Gaudium et Spes*

Non-Catholic observers of Vatican II kept positing questions about the Archdiocesan implementation of council documents through calling for responses to their many questions voiced in local newspapers: What was the effect of the use on English in the Mass on the prayer life of the laity? What was the St. Paul Archdiocese doing to improve relations between Catholics and Protestants? Was there a crisis in authority in the church? Why were the bishops so slow to speak out on such social issues as civil rights, the war in Vietnam, nuclear armaments? How important were laymen to the life of the church? What specific steps was the Archdiocese taking to implement the decrees of Vatican II? What had Pope Paul's Birth Control Commission, of which Binz was a member, done to deal with the population explosion which threatened the quality of life for so many parts of the world? Why was the Second Vatican Council needed? The Minneapolis Tribune was persistent in asking these kinds of questions. Satisfying answers were very slow to come. Individual priests, laymen and laywomen took the initiative to make the decrees of Vatican II real in their lives. They took to heart that they were Church and in conscience felt compelled to accept the challenges of Vatican II. The hierarchical structure of the Catholic Church had become less meaningful to them in their response to the directives of Jesus to live His Gospel message..

Nevertheless, administrative protocol was still operative. Reticent in pushing too hard for ecumenism in the Archdiocese, Binz nonetheless permitted priests to give homilies at ecumenical prayer services provided they not be given in a church sanctuary. He did, however, permit Colman Barry, O.S.B., president of St. John's University in Collegeville, to give the homily at an ecumenical prayer service for members of the Minnesota state Legislature, January 3, 1967. This took place in Christ Lutheran Church near the State Capitol in St. Paul with all members of the legislature having been invited. Nevertheless, Binz refused to grant permission to the Paulists at St. Lawrence Church in Minneapolis to conduct a series of ecumenical discussions between Catholic priests and non-Catholic ministers. Many efforts of Bishops Shannon and Lucker to get the laity and clergy involved in ecumenical affairs failed because of the decision of Binz to wait for further guidelines laid down by Rome or by commissions of the NCCB. When an Ecumenical Commission for the Archdiocese became a reality, it was Shannon who recommended inviting a nun theologian, a member of the Christian Brothers, and at least one layman and one laywoman to be appointed as members of the council. Shannon and Lucker continuously strove to get priests of the Archdiocese to become actively involved in ecumenical affairs.

"*Through* loyalty to conscience Christians are joined to others in the search for truth."

Gaudium et Spes

There were some positive signs that trends toward ecumenism could not go unnoticed. Right Reverend Monsignor Dillon represented Archbishop Binz at the installation of Reverend Melford S. Knutson as President of the Southeastern District of the American Lutheran Church which took place at Christ Lutheran Church in St. Paul. Monsignor Jerome Quinn was appointed head of the Archdiocesan Commission for Ecumenism and represented Binz at the consecration of the Greek Orthodox Church of St. George in St. Paul. Reverend Joseph Baglio acted as the archbishop's liaison with the Minnesota Council of Churches which sought archdiocesan cooperation in several activities. In 1967, in accordance with the guidelines set forth by the NCCB,

Binz petitioned the Sacred Congregation for the Doctrine of the Faith in Rome for permission for a Protestant minister to officiate at a mixed marriage in Holy Cross Catholic Church in Minneapolis. In 1968 Auxiliary Bishop Shannon and Dr. Alvin Rogness, president of Luther Theological Seminary in St. Paul, co-chaired sessions on theological dialogues concerning the nature of the Church, the Biblical concept of faith, and the role of the Bible in the Church. Sister Alberta Huber, C.S.J., president of the College of St. Catherine, led the prayer at the opening of the Minnesota State Legislature. Dialogue among theologians from different denominations kept ecumenical hopes alive in the region. One of the most divisive issues within the Catholic Church in the years

Church of St. Bartholomew

"Jesus Christ sanctified human ties, above all family ties, which are the basis of social structures."

Gaudium et Spes

following Vatican II was the birth control issue. The issue was removed from the agenda of the Council Fathers and was given for study and recommendation to a papal commission which would report to the pope himself. Thus Pope Paul VI issued a papal encyclical, *Humanae Vitae,* on this critical subject in 1968. There was

Stained glass window, Holy Family Church, Minneapolis

little publicity or speculation about the work of this papal commission before *Humanae Vitae* was made public. It was little known that Archbishop Binz served on this commission. Conscience issues among the clergy of the diocese over total compliance with the encyclical coupled with increased questioning of mandatory celibacy for the clergy prompted a number of defections among the clergy of the Archdiocese, including Bishop James Shannon. During the same period, the numbers of religious men and women leaving their religious congregations created problems for Catholic parishes and service institutions under archdiocesan auspices. *Humanae Vitae* received strong support from the Council of Catholic Men, the Council of Catholic Women, other Catholic organizations, and many individuals throughout the archdiocese. The local Planned Parenthood organization made the controversy more poignant by requesting money from federally funded

anti-poverty programs to operate clinics in order to supply birth control information and devices to the poor. Some members of the Minneapolis secular power structure were closely associated with Planned Parenthood both locally and nationally, so Archbishop Binz was reluctant to formally oppose Planned Parenthood's appeal for federal funds. He felt that a collision with them would serve their interests rather than those of Catholic Charities. The more pro-active agitation of Minnesota's Pro-Lifers against Planned Parenthood would come later.

During this time, the Archdiocesan Priests' Senate strove to implement necessary changes that the Council had recommended. The notion of the archbishop and his priests acting collegially in matters pertaining to local Church meant that there had to be continuous dialogue between the archbishop and his priests. In this spirit, a resolution was passed by the Priests' Senate on December 3, 1968 providing for due process regulations as related to Church Law. It had become evident that Canon Law proved inadequate in meeting the contemporary needs of the Church in the United States. This resolution was then forwarded to Archbishop Binz for formal adoption. The Midwest Regional Canon Law Society held a meeting in St. Paul in April, 1967. Topics discussed included: Religious and Local Ordinaries in the Post-Conciliar Period, the Quality of Law in the Post Vatican II Period, and the Lay Advocate in the Diocesan Tribunal.

The 1960s also saw our country torn apart by problems arising out of the Vietnam War. With growing opposition to American involvement in the war, many Catholic young men between the ages of 18 and 26 were confronted with a serious moral dilemma. Their consciences had been formed on a tradition of a just war but now they had to decide how to act in the face of a war they did not believe to be just. University and college campuses erupted with discontent over the draft and protest sit ins and marches. The youth of the archdiocese were swept into these times of discontent. Since occupational deferments from military service were eliminated, the options open to the men were, jail, emigration, violation of their consciences by participation in what they thought an unjust war, or perjuring themselves by declaring conscientious objection when they didn't really believe that all war was wrong. The U.S. bishops' statement on conscientious objection did not prove helpful. The men wanted the bishops to confront the president and Congress to pass a conscientious objector law for this specific war. Unwilling to do this, the bishops left the young men to their own decisions and actions. Discontent over the war grew within all age groups of society, marshalling behind the leadership of the SDS (Students for a Democratic Society). Priests, nuns, and laity joined the ranks of the protesters. Catholic groups within the archdiocese were sorely split over the issue of American involvement in Vietnam. This added to the growing distrust of Church authority.

Some ethnic disparities persisted in the region despite steps made toward

Archbishop Binz and the International Deaf Conference, 1972

integration. During the Eisenhower years the policy of the federal government encouraged the migration of American Indians from isolated reservations into urban areas to find decent jobs, decent homes, and a better life for their families. In 1965 there were about 8500 Indians in the Twin Cities. About 75 percent were Catholic. During the immediate years following and into the early 1970s this number grew dramatically as did awareness of outright racial prejudice against American Indians. The Minnesota Council of Churches and the Archdiocesan Catholic Charities collaborated in setting up the Newcomer Center in Minneapolis. The American Indian Movement consolidated during these years with headquarters in Minneapolis. Indian leaders, local priests, women religious, and committed lay people worked hard to get federal funds appropriated for building an adequate housing project in South Minneapolis for the city's homeless, most of whom were Indians. The Little Earth Housing Project was the result.

During the Civil Rights marches of the 1960s many priests, nuns, and lay men and women from the archdiocese marched in solidarity with Rev. Martin Luther King and the Black protesters. However, there was no official archdiocesan statement of support of the protesters' measures nor of condemnation of anti-integration methods used in Arkansas, Alabama, and other areas that supported Jim Crow measures. Neither were there steps taken to prohibit participation in those marches by priests, nuns, and others. This stance of the archdiocese angered some and pleased others. The NCCB did little more than condemn the use of violence.

After Vatican II lay leadership in the archdiocese, encouraged in the previous

episcopacies, assumed a different dimension. The works of the Knights of Columbus, Catholic Order of Foresters, Catholic Aid Society, the Catholic Women's Guild, Daughters of Isabella and others kept on with their insurance programs and myriads of fraternal activities. Many of these societies participated in an Interfaith Laymen's Ecumenical Encounter which took place at Gustavus Adolphus Lutheran College in St. Peter, Minnesota in August, 1965. On the national scene a group of men and women strove to organize a Lay Concilium to promote Catholic Action among the laity in the Spirit of Vatican II. Lay persons would form the central council and they in turn would instruct other lay leaders in various dioceses to implement actions at parish levels. This Concilium's primary goal was to instruct the greater faithful in the tenets of the Vatican II documents and lead in the implementing of them at all levels. The NCCB was leery of promoting such a group.

Church of St. Louis, Saint Paul

83

St. Paul Rosary Rally shatters crowd records

"*Individual and collective activity ... to improve the circumstances of the world ... corresponds to the plan of God.*"

Gaudium et Spes

Rosary Procession

In the archdiocese a federation of the major apostolic male organizations was formed in 1965. Called "The Archdiocesan Council of Catholic Men", this group had on its board of 18, six from St. Paul, six from Minneapolis, six from rural areas of the archdiocese and representatives from the Holy Name Society, Knights of Columbus, Confraternity of Christian Doctrine, Serra Club, Catholic Action groups acting as associate directors. The ACCM emphasized lay collaboration with the bishops and priests in the principal movements of renewal in the Church. It complied with the leadership of the National Confraternity of Catholic Men in pledging close cooperation with the American hierarchy, clergy, and religious

Opposing Page: Baldaquin Altar, St. Mary's Basilica

and not engage in conflicts with hierarchical decisions.

Christian renewal was at the heart of how Archbishop Binz assumed his pastoral role. The first Cursillo in the Archdiocese was held in 1968. This experience is a supernatural and natural means by which God brings to individuals a more conscious awareness of the indwelling of the Holy Spirit in themselves as well as in all those with whom they associate. The May Day Rosary Procession, started in the late 1940s, was continued during these years as a public proclamation of faith and of the Church's special love for the Blessed Mother. In 1975 this celebration was combined with a Holy Year Indulgence stressing the theme of reconciliation and renewal. Binz had long striven to have the Church elevate the rosary to a place alongside the Divine Office as an official prayer of the Church. He felt that many lay people could not make use of the Roman Breviary but still wanted to participate in the official public prayer of the Church. The Church had generally considered the rosary simply a private prayer. And so it has remained. The rosary processions to the Cathedral in St. Paul and St. Mary's Basilica in Minneapolis have been the faithful's public acclamation of Mary's role in the Catholic Church.

84

Stained glass window,
St. Hedwig Church,
Minneapolis

"The circumstances of life today have undergone such profound changes on the social and cultural level that one is entitled to speak of a new age of human history."

Gaudium et Spes

All Saints Church, Lakeville

New parishes accompanied the spread of the Twin Cities metropolitan ring of suburbia. Contemporary Church building architecture and art became more readily apparent here than in the inner cities with their established forms. Here, too, many functions of the parish heretofore the domain of the priests were increasingly provided by lay parishioners. When the issue of using state funds for busing parochial students arose in the mid-1960s, parents (Catholics, Lutherans, and others) formed a group called Citizens for Education, which was successful in bringing the school bus question into the political arena and won important concessions. As the costs of operating parochial schools skyrocketed, many parishes abandoned the schools and turned toward religious education programs run by the parishes. A new role, Director of Religious Education, appeared on the parish staffs. Adults in the parish, well trained in their faith, were called to serve as instructors in these programs. The archdiocesan Superintendent of Education now had more complex issues in consolidating Catholic education for the archdiocese. Increased costs and staffing problems of Catholic high schools in the area caused serious problems in that part of the Church's education ministry. By this time several new Catholic high schools had been built: Benilde, Hill, Brady, Archbishop Murray, Grace, and Regina High School. The older schools continued: St. Joseph's Academy, Cretin, Derham Hall, St, Thomas Academy, Our Lady of Peace, De La Salle, St. Margaret's, Holy Angels Academy, St. Agnes, and St. Bernard's. Various religious communities originally staffed these, but as religious defection grew, more and more lay instructors had to be hired. The costs of operating these institutions grew escalating tuition rates. This same phenomenon impacted the parish elementary schools. The Catholic laity more and more felt the strains of double taxation for educating their children. Many sent their children to public schools relying on parish religious education programs for necessary Catholic training, previously provided by the Catholic schools. The Confraternity

of Christian Doctrine, long a promoter of all forms of education in the Catholic faith, stressed the idea that the confraternity is fundamentally a parish organization requiring cooperation among pastors, religious, and laity in carrying out CCD projects. Aid to support archdiocesan educational programs came from many concerned lay groups besides the local parish groups and the annual Archbishop's Appeal Program. The Catholic Aid Association, a fraternal insurance group for Catholics, started a scholarship program to help defray Catholic college costs for students. Over the years this support was extended to Catholic parochial schools as well. Alumnae Associations of the region's Catholic high schools and colleges also adopted scholarship programs in order to help maintain the thrust for Catholic education in the archdiocese. The Catholic Athletic Association was organized to help schools and parishes

Church of the Epiphany, Coon Rapids

Church of St. Vincent de Paul, Saint Paul

develop athletic programs for children. This was seen as a means of channeling the energies of potential problem children. This association worked with schools, Catholic Charities, and with youth programs already begun by the Catholic Youth Centers of the Twin Cities. The archdiocese continued to be a strong supporter of the Catholic Boy Scouts through that organization's training ofCatholic men who would serve the Boy Scouts of America in a "Catholic Way." The boy was trained in scouting and in sound Catholic morals needed in the apostolate. The scout leader served God by serving the boy. There were awards, *Ad Altare* Medals, presented to worthy boys at an annual ceremony. There were no comparable programs for Catholic girls in the Girl Scout Program.

The Newman Center at the University of Minnesota had become a haven for students, priests, and concerned laity in general who desired innovations in the liturgy and more rapid implementation of the changes called for by Vatican II. When changes in the priest personnel were rumored, students warned that such action without consulting students would disrupt smooth operations at the center and give a wrong message to those students who participated in Newman activities. Adult supporters of Newman claimed that Newman liturgies reflected the idiom of the times and helped draw things together for participants. Newman had become known for its guitar Masses, informal garb of priest celebrants, dialogue homilies, and the reception of Holy Communion under both species. The form of worship that critics advocated used formality and dignity to set religion apart from the casual, informal life Americans were enjoying. The center's supporters asked Archbishop Binz to allow the priests of Newman the freedom to develop the liturgy that they had enjoyed in the past. Newman also sponsored lecture series on many controversial topics of the day, often sponsoring some of the most controversial speakers on these topics. Newman leaders insisted that young people's religious formation must grow in an atmosphere of both joy and intellectual inquiry. Changes in the priest personnel at Newman were made nonetheless.

Church of the Ascension, Minneapolis

"*T*he Gospel has aroused in the hearts of men an unquenchable thirst for human dignity."

Gaudium et Spes

The involvement of the Archdiocese in Catholic health care faced a host of problems during the post Vatican Council years. The abortion issue, drug culture, and advancements in medical science raised many ethical questions. The Catholic hospitals throughout the region were owned and operated by women religious dedicated to serve the Church yet enmeshed in organizational relationships with secular and governmental agencies, caught in the loops of rising hospital costs, and delicate relations with physicians and governing boards. Hospital chaplains required special training which put additional strain on a diminished pool of available priests in the archdiocese. The sisters at St. Mary's Hospital in Minneapolis met the need for nursing specialization by changing from a three-year School of Nursing Program to a two year junior college approach, giving an AA degree. St. Mary's Junior College not only addressed the nursing program, but also offered six other special services. These grew to 11 by 1968. The hospitals would still be resources for the clinical education needed for the degrees. The hospital chaplaincy need took a giant step forward when Father William Kenny became qualified in Clinical Pastoral Education, a program accredited by the National Association of Catholic Chaplains and authorized

by the Catholic University of America. Kenny worked to get others, men and women, accredited for this special work. This chaplaincy program was all under the auspices of the United States Catholic Conference, Washington, D.C. It was imperative that the sisters and growing number of Catholic laypersons on hospital boards work closely to maintain the strong Catholic mission of the hospitals.

In 1966 the official title of the archdiocese became "The Archdiocese of St. Paul and Minneapolis." The apostolic activities of the archdiocese continued in myriad forms as special needs became the special ways of bringing Christ to those in need for certain individuals who championed the causes. Care for retarded children, long a work in Faribault, saw new programs sponsored by the Catholic Charities, the metropolitan Catholic Hospitals, and especially the Christ Child School in St. Paul. Archbishop Binz wanted these groups to participate in the state's programs for the retarded. The Conventual Franciscan Fathers and Benedictines staffed the Glen Lake School for Boys, a correctional facility under the jurisdiction of Catholic Charities.

In 1965 the Catholic Interracial Council of the Twin Cities began a program of assisting minority youngsters attend Catholic high schools under an educational grant program. Grantees were chosen for the program on academic ability and the promise of leadership potential. Parishes of the Archdiocese participated in a program called "Black Catholics Concerned", which worked with the National Office for black Catholics in Washington, D.C. for safeguarding the rights of blacks in America and striving to obliterate discrimination against blacks. Funds for these endeavors were handled through the chancery. Roy Wilkins sought financial support from the archdiocese for the NAACP in St. Paul in its struggle to bring equal justice and educational opportunity to blacks in St. Paul. Non-whites were demanding their constitutional rights in education, housing, and politics as well. The archdiocese also supported the Mexican-American Cultural Center in San Antonio Texas, which proved to be most helpful to priests, sisters, seminarians and deacons working with the Spanish-speaking Catholics in the United States. The work of Sister Giovanni, SSND, with St. Paul's Hispanic community on St. Paul's West Side kept the needs of that minority group ever before the offices of the archdiocese as well as the state.

Church of St. Edward, Bloomington

Saint Paul Seminary campus

*"*H*is command to the apostles was to preach the Gospel to all people in order that the human race would become the family of God, in which love would be the fulness of the law."*

Gaudium et Spes

The global dimension of missionary work had an impact on local thinking and priority setting. Missionaries from all over the globe were allowed to speak and solicit funds for their works. Help was given to various religious groups working in Mexico, South America, Africa, India, Korea, Alaska, Communist East Europe, and the Far East. Archbishop Binz was a great supporter of the Catholic League for Religious Assistance to Poland. He asked for generous contributions to the League to support Polish seminaries in Rome and Paris and their aid to oppressed Catholics in Lithuania. There Catholics were fighting for a minimum of freedom of worship in a struggle with the Soviets. In 1967 the archdiocese sponsored four Papal Volunteers for Christian work of development in Latin America. The role of these laymen was to infuse the spirit of the gospel into the various

communities and spheres of life that they served. The National Headquarters for Papal Volunteers was in Chicago. The immediate need was for men and women with competence and skill in fields of education, health care, agriculture, cooperatives, technology, and social work.

The modern communication explosion forced the archdiocese into debates that extended beyond local into national and international concerns. The archbishop strove to garner support for the Catholic Radio and Television Association (CARTA), whose headquarters were in New York City. The plan was to

Resurrection Statue, Saint Paul Seminary

Church of St. Joseph the Worker, Maple Grove

Shrine,
Saint Paul
Seminary

organize a diocesan radio and television office in the archdiocese. A lay board of advisors would plan for religious programing for youth, ecumenical programing, uses and methods of educational TV, and the awarding of CARTA grants for local programing. Catholic fraternals were asked to participate in the Foundation Plan of CARTA. The program never really got off the ground. Binz never wanted to get involved with *Catholic*

Digest business, although local priests had long been involved in its publication and international growth.

A move for St. Paul's cooperation with other seminaries in the region took place in 1965 when the Upper Midwest Association of Seminary College Departments was organized. This was to be a structure for mutual help in studying ways of improving standards and of coordinating the pre-theological studies with the developing programs of the theological schools. Standing committees were set up to work on areas of common concern. The Episcopal Conference on Priestly Training and the Conference of Major Superiors of Men were informed of this new organization.

92

"*Every group must take into account the needs and legitimate aspirations of every other group, and still more of the human family as a whole.*"

Gaudium et Spes

With all of the changes the society faced in the 1960s and 1970s, the stress on family life was a major concern. The Christian Family Movement, headquartered in Chicago, had a council in St. Paul. It aimed to address problems facing families in living out the mandates of the Gospel amid all the societal and church changes taking place. In August, 1966 the CFM area convention was held at the College of St. Catherine. Experts in a variety of fields were invited as presenters on topics including: The Constitution on the Church, the family in relationship, the family and economics, responsible parenting, teenagers and responsibility, industry and profits in Christian living, the shrinking farms, laymen's responsibility in implementing Vatican II, prayers in the home, formation of the young, racial justice, the St. Paul Diocese, Sisters in the CFM groups, and leadership training.

The Rural Life Committee of the archdiocese became an active arm of the Rural Life Conference, the Catholic National Farmers Organization. This group addressed the plight of the farmers in light of *Mater et Magistra* and sought collective efforts at achieving agrarian justice. It sought theological advisors to guide farmers in moral decisions they must make. They called for all priests to make a study of the NFO and to be supportive in seeking formal legislation to protect the farming minority in a time when major attention was focused on urban sprawl and the needs of a burgeoning metropolitan population. The Rural Life Conference called for the development of rural professionalism among rural people at the grass roots level. The archdiocese sponsored an institute at the College of St. Thomas to address these issues.

*Rural Life
Day Mass*

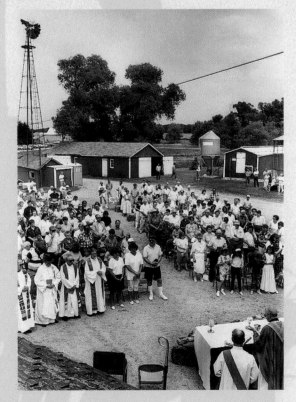

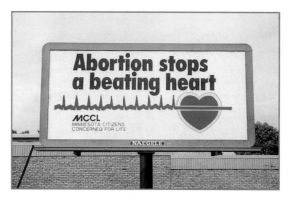

"*The sublime dignity of the human person who stands above all things and whose rights and duties are universal and inviolable.*"

Gaudium et Spes

Minnesota Citizens Concerned for Life billboard

The justice issues raised in Mater et Magistra prompted a genuine concern for the rights of the working class within the metropolitan area. Justice in the workplace became a major issue. Archbishop Binz appointed Rt. Rev. Msgr. Francis J. Gilligan, Pastor of the Church of St. Mark in St. Paul, as his official representative at the Religion and Labor Luncheons which were rejuvenated. These affairs were organized in order to keep religious leaders apprised of the concerns of labor. Because priests worked so closely with their parishioners, the AFL-CIO sought their assistance in many disputes. Local unions trusted and sought the help of Msgr. Gilligan as arbiter in settling many local labor disputes.

Monsignor Gilligan and Kay O'Keefe, Confraternity of Catholic Women meeting

March for Life, St. Paul Capitol

During the final years of the Binz episcopate, the Right to Life Movement became more vocal in the archdiocese. The Minnesota Citizens Concerned for Life (MCCL), under the presidency of Marjory Mecklenburg, became a strong citizen lobby in Minnesota resulting in a public policy in favor of life, These pro-lifers strove to protect the right to life of all human beings, particularly the unborn, the aged, the mentally retarded, the handicapped, and other disadvantaged and vulnerable persons. There was also support given to the Couple to Couple League which aimed to provide leadership training in natural family planning.

Pro-life demonstration

> ## "*It is up to everyone to see to it that woman's specific and necessary participation in cultural life be acknowledged and fostered.*"
>
> *Gaudium et Spes*

Many of these issues became enmeshed in women's groups that were seeking forums for their voices calling for justice for women in the Church. These sought help from the United States Center of Concern in Washington, D.C. Appealing to the Committee on Social Development and World Peace, the focus of justice for women expanded to world justice issues. Women and men religious united in their support of this. They called for the study of theological foundations and social justice aspects of the Women's Movement with the hope to contribute to the discussions and decisions of the United Nations International Year. They worked on problems related to hunger, population, and resources in a world divided between the rich and the poor.

Bishops throughout the country were asked for support. Archbishop Binz withheld archdiocesan support while awaiting some official response from the NCCB. His poor health had forced him to miss many meetings of the bishops so he had little knowledge of the

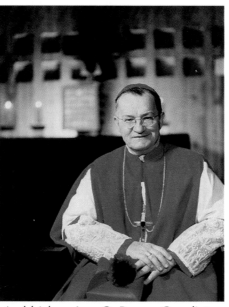

Archbishop Leo C. Byrne, Coadjutor

Pectoral Cross and ring of Archbishop Leo C. Byrne

discussions that had been taking place.

Archbishop Binz's poor health prompted his requesting a coadjutor archbishop for the archdiocese. In 1967 Archbishop Leo C. Byrne, former Auxiliary Bishop of St. Louis, became the Coadjutor Archbishop of St. Paul and Minneapolis. Archbishop Binz retired in 1975 and died in 1979.

LEO C. BYRNE was appointed Coadjutor Archbishop with the right of succession for the St. Paul and Minneapolis Archdiocese, on August 2, 1967. Born on March 19, 1908 in St. Louis, Missouri, Byrne attended Kenrick Seminary and was ordained June 10, 1933. With advance degrees in sociology and social work, he was known for his work as pastor and in Catholic Charities in St. Louis. He was appointed Auxiliary to the Archbishop of St. Louis in 1954 and Coadjutor Bishop of Wichita, Kansas in 1961 before coming to St. Paul. In 1969 he was chosen consulter for the Bishops' Commission on the Liturgy. In 1971 he participated in the World Synod of Bishops in Rome and that same year was elected Vice-President of the United States Catholic Conference and the National Council of Catholic Bishops.

"*The arms race is one of the greatest curses on the human race.*"

Gaudium et Spes

Early in his administration, he voiced his hatred of war and prayed for peace. The Minneapolis Catholic Youth Center sponsored an anti-war and conscription panel. Byrne declined the invitation to attend this gathering. The assembled throng drafted an anti-Vietnam War letter and several priests and women religious signed the protest statement which was subsequently sent to Congress in Washington, D.C. This group of protesters held a rally at the First Universalist Church in Minneapolis. They sang peace and freedom songs and heard anti-war and anti-draft speeches. These activities prompted 17 clergymen in the Twin Cities to turn in their draft cards. One of these priests protested before the United States embassy in Saigon and was arrested in Rome and in Washington, D. C., for activities of trying to conduct peace marches. He ultimately became a coordinator of the International Assembly of Christians, a group that sought solidarity with the Vietnamese, Laotian and Cambodian people, in protesting America's involvement in the war. These protesters did not receive archdiocesan support. Archdiocesan leaders did not want to be accused of fostering un-American activities.

Archbishop Byrne championed the validity of the Catholic School System and its enormous contribution to the development of the Church and let it be known he would not turn his back on Catholic education just because of financial and personnel shortages. He lauded the Second Vatican Council and stressed that it made no changes in Church dogma. He noted that many regulations were Church laws, not dogma, and could be changed. He believed that married deacons were a

possible approach to solving the shortage of priests. He ardently worked for liberating legislation for the oppressed through his endorsement of the Joint Religious Legislative Coalition and its work for social justice. He committed the archdiocese to a campaign to Save the Cities, which made funds available in an effort to prevent further decay of the metropolitan core cities. He established a Board of Investment Ethics to review the portfolio of the archdiocese and to influence change in those corporations which in any way subordinated people for profit. The Code of Ethical Guidelines devised by this group, led by Monsignor Ambrose Hayden, Episcopal Vicar, was the most comprehensive of any among the dioceses of the United States at the time. Byrne clearly supported the rights of workers and was an advocate of workers organizing their own unions. As a champion of justice, he received the Archbishop John Ireland Distinguished Service award in 1974.

Monsignor Ambrose Hayden

"Faith with its solidly based teaching, provides every thoughtful person with an answer to his anxious queries about his future lot.*"*

Gaudium et Spes

The archbishop was called on to address many social issues which lay leaders wanted him as Church leader to address. The St. Mary's Hospital treatment center for alcoholics had retained the Johnson Institute, led by an Episcopalian clergyman, for counseling, group therapy, and other non-medical portions of the proposed treatment. When the hospital asked that Father Arnold Luger,who had two years experience in the area of 5th Step counseling and pastoral care, come to St. Mary's as a trainee in the pioneering program, Archbishop Byrne refused the request. He felt the priest shortage necessitated assigning priests to parish work primarily. Nevertheless, the work of Dr. George Mann and others at St. Mary's became nationally known for its success with recovering alcoholics.

At the same time Byrne addressed the issue of alcoholism and drug dependency among priests. Recognizing these afflictions as illnesses, he drew up a policy for dealing with these problems. An evaluation committee, composed of clerical and lay persons who were knowledgeable in the field of chemical dependency and imbued with a sense of Christian charity, was set up. Committed to absolute confidentiality, the committee would serve as a source of information to archdiocesan clergy, providing them with the necessary literature on the disease and methods of its treatment. All expense of treatment and work of the committee would be assumed by the archdiocese. The Hazelden Treatment Center in Lindstrom, Minnesota had served the needs of priests, brothers, and sisters over the years. The archdiocese provided funds to advance the work of Hazelden.

Issues like getting Christ into the communication media and making Christ a presence in the homes for the aged were supported and promoted by the local Knights of Columbus. Byrne was an avid supporter of the Minnesota Governor's Council on Aging and provided additional funding through archdiocesan support. The Knights also addressed the demands of the John Birch Society for public forums in the region. Because of the prevailing fear of Communism, many local Catholics supported this group.

Statue from St. Mary's Basilica, Minneapolis

"It is to be hoped that more of the laity will receive adequate theological formation and that some among them will dedicate themselves professionally to these studies and contribute to their advancement."

Gaudium et Spes

Byrne felt strongly that it was necessary to have cooperation between Catholic theologians and bishops and worked toward the development of cooperation between the National Council of Catholic Bishops and the Catholic Theological Society. A cooperative venture between these two groups resulted in the document, "Basic Doctrines for Catholic Religious Education," which explored the possibility of Catholic membership in the National Council of Churches, the question of the place of women in the Church, the permanent diaconate, providing theologians as resource persons for regional meetings of bishops, and drawing up ethical directives for hospitals. This thrust emphasized the role of theologians in the service of the American Church.

Another step in the archdiocese to involve the laity more directly in local Church affairs was the setting up of the Pastoral Council. On August 25, 1972 Archbishop Byrne convened the first meeting of the Council with membership including the archbishop, 24 lay persons, five priests, two sisters, and one brother.

Lay members were selected by parishes. Priests, sisters, and Brothers were selected by their respective groups. The Pastoral Council would act as an advisory group in archdiocesan affairs.

It was during the episcopacy of Byrne that steps were taken to reorganize the deaneries of the archdiocese. Although priests were concerned about a structure that would limit their freedom in any way, they did welcome a structure that would provide better communication and fellowship with fellow priests and with the chancery. A deanery system could serve that purpose. When Archbishop Byrne met with the deans to further this restructuring, issues discussed included the final configuration of deaneries, an insurance study for archdiocesan parishes, consideration of a priests' retirement home, continuing education of priests, and pastoral considerations.

The great migration from core cities to the suburbs continued throughout the 1960's and 1970's. The counterpart of this for the metropolitan area was that the core

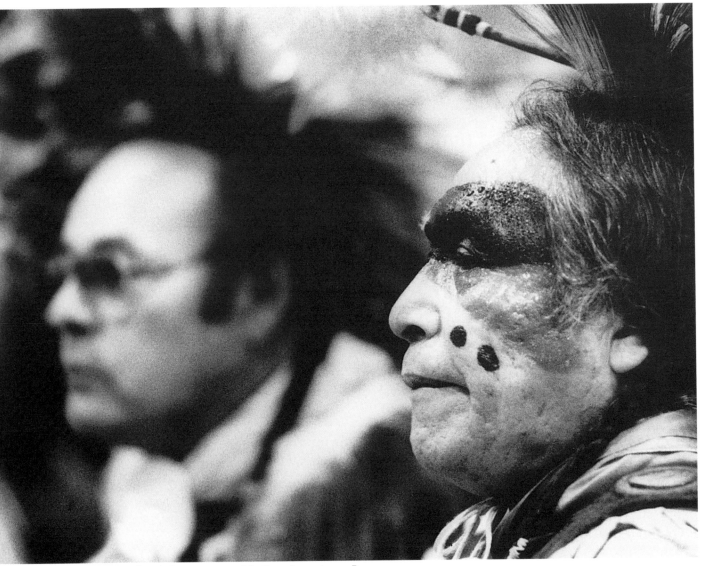

Participants at a Native American Pow-wow

cities' minorities and the concentration of the marginalized poor in St. Paul and Minneapolis created needs that the archdiocese had to address. Minneapolis had become a haven for Indians moving from hard times on the reservations hoping to better their lives in the metropolitan area. Priests and sisters at the parishes of Holy Rosary and St. Stephen led the way in organizing groups to provide food, shelter, health, and employment needs for this group. When the American Indian Movement headquarters moved to Minneapolis, the archdiocese donated grants to the movement's causes. It also contributed funds for emergency relief to those people affected by the controversy between the Indians and the federal government at Wounded Knee, South Dakota. The Priests' Senate recommended an Inter-City Urban Ministry for the archdiocese to help in the housing concerns in the Twin Cities. The St. Paul Housing and Redevelopment Authority was anxious to cooperate with the diocese in such a program.

"We are witnessing the birth of a new humanism, where man is defined before all else by his responsibility to his brother and at the court of history."

Gaudium et Spes

The independent initiative of Church people did not wait for archdiocesan leadership to address the needs of the neighbor which became marked by the economic and power-based differences between the affluent middle class and those on the fringes of society. Priests, nuns, and other Catholic laity collaborated with other Christian groups to support addressing these needs. The House of Charity in Minneapolis, the Dorothy Day Center in St. Paul, the Loaves and Fishes Program supported by many local parishes provided food and some shelter for the growing number of indigents in the cities. Alliance of the City attempted to help the street people become organized in order to better their lot. Nuns and priests championed the cause of the Indians in their fight for federal funds to build the Little Earth Housing Project in South Minneapolis. The St. Vincent de Paul Society, and a number of store fronts run independently by nuns and lay people continued to work in providing clothing and other needs for the poor. A groups of nuns, committed to fight for women's rights, started a shelter for battered women and provided protection and legal counsel for these abused women who had fallen through the cracks in the American legal system. Shelters for children on the run were also opened in an attempt to steer youths from the drug culture of the streets. The archdiocese continued to strengthen its long involvement in ministering to the deaf community. For almost 20 years the deaf community had

Dorothy Day Center, Saint Paul

Church of the Immaculate Conception, Columbia Heights

used the Newman Center at the University of Minnesota as their place of worship and social functions. A Program for the Deaf Youth of the Twin cities was inaugurated in 1974. Father Bill Kenney said a Mass in sign language twice a month for the deaf Catholic group and the archdiocese employed a sister full-time to work as religious education coordinator for the deaf. At this time the archdiocese relied heavily on outside agencies to help meet the needs of various handicapped and marginalized groups.

Preparing meals for the homeless

The lack of support for addressing the needs of homosexuals by the archdiocese brought harsh criticism and bad publicity in the press. An amendment to the St. Paul City Charter was proposed to the City Council which included a prohibition against discrimination because of sexual preference. The issue came to a head over the question of hiring homosexual teachers. In a letter to the mayor of St. Paul, Archbishop Byrne urged the City Council to vote against the amendment. He feared that homosexuals in such sensitive positions would undermine the common good and weaken American society in the long run. The archbishop avoided public confrontation with his opponents but reiterated the historic stance of the Catholic Church- condemn the sin but not the sinner. This brought media attacks of Archbishop Byrne and Monsignor Boxleitner, head of Catholic Welfare Services of Minneapolis, as supporters of blatant intolerance in their treatment of gay and lesbian people.

Gail Graiewski-Moore interprets Mass in sign language

In October, 1969 the Canon Law Society of America called for the institution of a Due Process Policy to be implemented in every diocese in the nation. A special committee comprised of representatives from the priests' senates in all of the bishoprics in the Metropolitan Province formulated a suggested procedure based on the principles of conciliation and arbitration. A three-tiered system of boards was to be used. A Conciliation Board would first hear the case. If this failed it would go to an Arbitration Board. A Review Board would handle legal actions needed if the other boards failed to bring the case to a satisfactory conclusion. This system became operative in the archdiocese in the fall of 1972.

The shortage of priests in the archdiocese was a major concern of Archbishop Byrne. Assistant priests in parishes became a thing of the past for most pastors. Many laity resented attempts to merge parishes, both in the metropolitan and rural areas. At the same time there was a call for chaplains to serve detention and correction facilities as well as ministers to the growing number of college campuses in the region. Byrne supported priests who served as volunteers in the Amicus Program, a befriender program for prison inmates. The resumed worker-priest program in France influenced some of the American clergy to pursue ministries to the poor outside the structures of the parish. The call for priests to serve in foreign lands was very strong. Archbishop Byrne was instrumental in collaborating with the Episcopal Conference of Guatemala in founding the National Major Seminary of Guatemala. He was awarded a certificate of honor in Asuncion in December, 1971 for his part in this venture. Byrne kept alive his plan for a priests' retirement home in the archdiocese and in 1974 he authorized a proposal for such a facility.

Amid this reality the question of the ordination of women came to the fore. The Episcopal Church's House of Bishops sought input from Archbishop Byrne about the attitudes of members of

Pornography protest

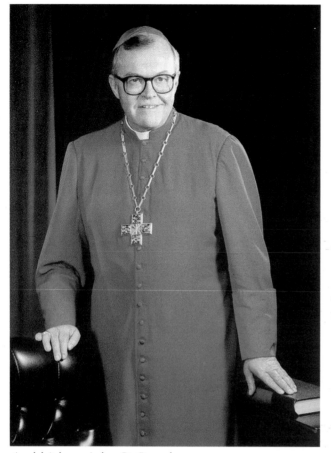

Archbishop John R. Roach

Bishop Raymond Lucker

the Catholic faith in the archdiocese about this issue. Byrne served as the chair of the National Bishops' Committee of Women in Society and in the Church. He maintained that the matter of discrimination toward women should be honestly viewed by members of society in the fields of education, government, business, and industry as justice issues. He also advocated that the Church should study the whole area of women in ministry. The archdiocese, however, was slow in addressing this issue. When the National Association of Women Religious met in Minneapolis in May, 1972, Byrne feared open confrontation with members of NAWR who were pushing for proactive measures from the U.S. Conference of Bishops on the issue of the ordination of women. Nevertheless, the archbishop had a good experience with the NAWR group.

On September 8, 1971, Raymond Lucker and John Roach were consecrated

auxiliary bishops in the Cathedral of St. Paul. This came at an appropriate time because in December, 1971 Archbishop Byrne was selected as vice president of the United States Council of Bishops. This meant he would have to spend much time away from the archdiocese. He had represented his brother bishops at the Synod of Bishops in Rome earlier that summer. Topics discussed included the ministerial priesthood and social justice, and Byrne who was a talented social psychologist proved to be most helpful. He believed that his duties as a bishop demanded that he assist his brother bishops and be interested, above all, in the universal Church.

"God has entrusted to all the noble mission of safeguarding life."

Gaudium et Spes

Perhaps the most controversial issue of Archbishop Byrne's episcopacy centered around the papal encyclical, *Humanae Vitae*. There was much publicized dissent from a number of theologians as well as members of the United States hierarchy who felt they could not accept, interiorly and exteriorly, all that the encyclical contained. These raised many questions regarding the role of the individual conscience, the scientific question of when life really begins, the purpose of marriage as more than having children, and parental responsibility of providing adequately for their children. More than 70 priests of the archdiocese signed a statement of dissent with *Humanae Vitae* and submitted it to their archbishop. Byrne then sent letters to all clergy in the archdiocese appealing to their loyalty to the Holy Father by fully supporting *Humanae Vitae*. He noted that submission of mind and will must be shown in a special way to the authentic teaching authority of the Roman Pontiff even when he is not speaking *ex cathedra*. He noted that professional and competent theologians would rightly debate and discuss the document but should adhere to the principles laid down in *Humanae Vitae*. Camps were formed, both in confirmation and dissent with this directive. Some clergy who felt they could not in conscience fully comply relinquished the priesthood completely. Auxiliary Bishop James Shannon was one of this group.

When the Supreme Court decision, Roe vs Wade, was issued in 1973, Archbishop Byrne was shocked that the taking of the life of a fetal person would be condoned. He declared this stance to be immoral. He thought the decision represented bad logic and bad law and noted the inconsistency of the highest court in the land which had just declared capital punishment unconstitutional. In his letter to the people of the archdiocese which appeared in the *Catholic Bulletin* he criticized the Supreme Court and placed the issue of abortion in its proper context: respect for life and spiritual values surrounding life. He called for the Church to make strong efforts to promote positive values respecting life in all areas of society. At the same time, as a pastor, he called for personal compassion for all without diluting the strength of the teaching of the Church.

Catholic Bulletin article on Humanae Vitae

Pope reaffirms birth control rejection

By JAMES C. O'NEILL

VATICAN CITY — (NC) — Pope Paul has confirmed the traditional teaching the Catholic church of family regulation has reaffirmed the rejection of every m of artificial birth control.

n an encyclical entitled Humanae Vi-, from the two Latin opening words, aning Of Human Life, Pope Paul in- ted on the norm of natural law that ach of every marriage act must remain n to the transmission of life."

Though not specifically mentioned the of the "pill" to avoid pregnancy is luded by the papal document, accord- to Msgr. Ferinando Lambruschini of me's Lateran university, who presented encyclical at a press conference Mon- y at the Vatican press hall.

Msgr. Lambruschini, a professor of ral theology, said that the encyclical, ile not infallible, nevertheless is an thentic pronouncement of the ordinary gisterium (teaching authority) of the urch and therefore Catholics must give "loyal and full assent."

The Roman moral theologian noted that he faithful know that the pope, the ccessor of St. Peter and the Vicar of rist, has a special assistance of the ly Ghost when going with the mission confirming in the faith and in the ys of the Lord all the members of e people of God, including the brothers

MSGR. FERNINANDO LAMBRUSCHINI

in the episcopate. This assistance does not restrict itself to infallible defini- tions. ...

"The pronouncement has come. It is not infallible but does not leave the ques- tions concerning birth regulation in a con- dition of vague problematics. The assent of theological faith is due only to the definitions properly so-called infallible, but there is owed also loyal and full assent, interior and not only exterior, to an authentic pronouncement of the magisterium, in proportion to the level of the authority from which it emanates — which in this case is the supreme authority of the Supreme Pontiff — and its object, which is most weighty since it is a matter of tormented question of the regulation of births."

Msgr. Lambruschini continued: "Those who in recent times uncautiously believed, even in good faith, that they could teach the lawfulness of using artificial contra- ceptive practices for the regulation of births and behaved accordingly in pas- toral directives and in the ministry of confession, must change their views and give the example by full adhesion to the teachings of the encyclical. It is not a question of deplorable servility but a necessary loyalty and consistency in the profession of Catholic teaching and in the practice of the Christian life."

as a weakness of content. That there can be no recourse to the subtle distinc- tion between the magisterium for the Ro- man diocese and the universal magisteri- um of the universal pontiff is evidenced by the fact that the encyclical is ad- dressed to all the bishops, priests and faithful of the church and to all men of good will, thus committing their con- sciences."

Msgr. Lambruschini, in the course of his press conference, said that biblical citations had been avoided largely be- cause there exists a controversy among exegetes (scholars who interpret biblical texts) on many passages. Instead, the encyclical is based on the norms of the natural law and not on revelation, he said.

Another moral theologian, the Rev. Francis Furlong, SJ, of the Jesuits' Mis- souri province, a professor at Rome's Gregorian university, pointed out that the pope's document has cut through the dis- agreements of theologians and other learned men.

"Here you have a striking example of the need we have for a church that can teach with authority. We have seen how great men and great minds meeting to- gether and discussing together have not been able to come up with a unanimous, definite, acceptable solution to the prob- lem of contraception.

"We can and should be most grateful to God that he has established a teaching

POPE PAUL VI

church which can tell us authoritative and with certainty what we must belie and what we must do in order to atte eternal life."

Pope Paul acknowledged that "it c be foreseen that this teaching will perha

(Continued on Page 19)

Responsibility called grave

CASTELGANDOLFO — (NC) — Pope ul VI said Wednesday that his sense "grave responsibility" caused him "no all spiritual suffering" in the four years study that preceded issuance of the cyclical on family regulation and birth ntrol.

"Today we wish to speak to you, the elings that filled our heart during the ng period of preparation of our en- clical Humanae Vitae," the pope told general audience." The knowledge of r grave responsibility caused us no all suffering."

"We will know of the heated discussions the press. The anguish of those involved the problem touched us also. We studied d read all we could. We consulted emi- nt persons. We sought, in prayer, the of the Holy ...

The Catholic BULLETIN

Archdiocesan Edition

Vol. 58, No. 31   Copy 12c, Year $5   Friday, Aug. 2, 1968

"*Christians ... should actively strive to promote the values of marriage and the family.*"

Gaudium et Spes

The National Conference of Catholic Bishops established the Human Life Foundation and sponsored the First World Conference on Natural Family Planning in January, 1971. The foundation opened offices in Washington, D.C. and called for collaboration of all experts, Catholics and all others, regarding life issues. It also advised that local diocesan offices be established. In the archdiocese of St. Paul and Minneapolis, Byrne helped set up a Natural Family Planning Program. However these efforts paled in the light of the millions of dollars spent by world governments and private agencies endorsing contraception, sterilization, and abortion. Massive birth control propaganda by Planned Parenthood and the World Bank flooded the country, reaching every local parish in the archdiocese.

The Catholic hospitals of the Twin Cities were thrust into the maelstrom of diverse opinions regarding this right to life issue, particularly since health care facilities had moved into a cooperative mode regarding sharing cost-saving procedures. Maternity patients, after delivery in a Catholic facility, were reported to transfer to a neighboring hospital for tubal ligations and then return to the Catholic facility for further health care. Non-Catholic doctors approved of this system since many of

the patients they brought to the Catholic hospital ethically justified these procedures. Questions surrounding medical ethics surmounted as transplant surgery and new methods of prolonging life were advanced. This region of the country had long been known for being avant-garde in the area of health care and initiating cooperative ventures among area hospitals toward health care improvement. How to advance the Catholic philosophy of sacredness of life at all stages of life in such a milieu while at the same time further progress within the health care professions was very difficult. Archbishop Byrne kept close contact with the boards of the Catholic hospitals and addressed the Catholic Hospital Association on Catholic principles of the right to life at its 54th Convention held in Minneapolis. He actively supported the Kidney Transplant Program of the University of Minnesota Hospital and appointed a priest to the hospital apostolate ministry there. Pressed by the laity, he set up a hospital chaplaincy program to counteract the impersonal approach of many parish priests who were not trained to work with the sick and who had been visiting hospitals as just one more pastoral duty.

Archbishop Byrne moved the Catholic Church in the Minnesota region toward friendlier relations between Catholic and Protestant clergymen. The thrust toward ecumenism called for by Vatican II moved ever so slowly in the archdiocese. To lay the foundations for the "thaw" that would help melt the 400 year old Protestant-Catholic cold war, Pope John XXIII had created the Secretariat for Christian Unity. The Council had said that organic union was not the purpose of the Ecumenical Movement, but rather to grow in spiritual understanding and oneness. The world called for greater understanding and cooperation among all Christian people - Protestant, Orthodox, and Catholic. Archbishop Byrne organized an Ecumenical Commission and charged it to draw up guidelines for ecumenism in the archdiocese. Urged by Bishop James Shannon and Father Jerome Quinn, the archbishop enlarged the membership of the commission to include besides clergy, six members of the laity and representatives of men and women religious of the diocese. In compliance with the Roman Directory, this commission drew up guidelines, covering areas wherein cooperation could take place: prayer in common, worship in common, Protestants could be welcomed guests and witnesses at baptism and confirmation, mixed marriages between Catholics and other Christians could now take place during Mass, and Christians of other faiths could be witnesses in marriage ceremonies. Separated fellow

Christians were not permitted to join in the sacramental actions of Eucharist, Penance and Anointing. As early as 1969 people were asking permission for "intercommunion" but Lutherans shared many of the Catholics' reservations on this sharing in the reception of the Eucharist. Both groups felt that a long road had yet to be traveled before the respective Churches could in conscience assure their members that differences with others were only ritual ones.

Archbishop Byrne worked closely with the Minneapolis Council of Churches and worked with leaders of other faiths in the Joint Religious Legislative Coalition, which brought closer ties with the Jewish leaders in the area. The Beth El Congregation of Minneapolis praised Archbishop Byrne for his championing understanding between the various religions and races which had won deep respect of all. The archdiocese provided personnel and funds to cooperate with the Center for Urban Encounter, an

Archbishop Leo C. Byrne attends ceremony of installation of Ukrainian bishop, Church of St. Constantine

Church of St. Constantine, Minneapolis

Archbishop Roach confers with Lutheran bishops

ecumenical program for training Church leadership for social change in the Twin cities. Archbishops Binz and Byrne participated in the Minnesota Study Committee for Christian Cooperation held at Northwestern Lutheran Theological Seminary in St. Paul in February, 1973. This was a joint study of possible membership in the Minnesota Council of Churches. Yet, the archbishops were reluctant to join the Minnesota Council of Churches, which was aggressive in developing avenues of Christian cooperation, both locally and nationally.

Fourth Anniversary of Lutheran-Catholic Covenant

Other groups were working hard for ecumenism. The monks at St. John's Abbey in Collegeville had long

striven for ecumenical and liturgical advancement. Their Institute for Ecumenical and Cultural Research at the Abbey was internationally known. Theologians and scholars were drawn to the institute, contributing to the work of the Church through Liturgical Press publications in worship and Gospel living called for by Vatican II. Not only was the Institute wholeheartedly supported by Archbishop Byrne but it also became the beneficiary of the Patrick Butler Family of St. Paul, who received papal acknowledgement for its largesse. The Benedictine priests and sisters continued to be great supporters of various ministries of the Church in the archdiocese and strong ties with Collegeville continued.

> *"*C*atholics will seek to cooperate actively and positively with our separated brethren, who profess the charity of the Gospel along with us, and also with those thirsting for true peace."*
>
> *Gaudium et Spes*

Liturgical concerns raised by the laity demanded pastoral decisions. Differences among the parishes in handling these concerns caused some confusion among the laity and letters deluged the chancery offices. There was disagreement over whether or not bishops could permit the reception of Holy Communion more than once a day, the practice of receiving Holy Communion in the hand, and the role of extraordinary ministers of the Eucharist. Liturgical concerns of the radicals found their way into resolutions sent to the Federation of Diocesan Liturgical Commission: that women should be ordained, that bishops should be elected, that there be no age, marriage, or celibacy restrictions for deacons, and that no church should be built unless it be a multi-purpose building. Another issue of concern was how would pastors minister to and address the problems of the divorced and remarried Catholics in their parishes? This was certainly an issue that needed to be addressed by the entire Church, not just the Archdiocese of St. Paul and Minneapolis. In the interim, Archbishop Byrne felt fortunate that his

Archishop John R. Roach

see had one of the best marriage tribunals in the country.

On October 21, 1974 Archbishop Leo C. Byrne died quite suddenly. When he did not appear for his 8 a.m. Mass, the sisters went to awaken him and found him lying across his bed dead. For seven years he served the people of the archdiocese with generosity and attentive concern. He had become known for his simple faith, dedication to prayer, and open, cheerful leadership. His episcopacy was marked with his commitment to social justice and reconciliation, his witness to the value of human life, and his work to strengthen Catholic life and institutions. He was remembered especially as the founder of the Pastoral Council and as a leader who dealt with all in the archdiocese as a friend.

Archbishop Leo Binz relinquished his peaceful retirement in order to administer the archdiocese until a new archbishop could be appointed. Binz, not well himself and taken aback by Byrne's sudden death, was aided by the administrative skills of Monsignor

110

Ambrose Hayden, the vicar general of the archdiocese.

JOHN ROACH was named Archbishop in 1975 when Archbishop Binz stepped down. The new archbishop of St. Paul and Minneapolis was someone who knew the region very well. John Roach was born on July 31, 1921 in Prior Lake, Minnesota. At that time this was a village of about 500 just to the southwest of Minneapolis where his parents ran a general store. They taught John and his two younger sisters that their local church of St. Michael was very important in their lives. John learned from a veterinarian neighbor great respect for all of God's creatures. After attending high school in Shakopee, he entered Nazareth Hall and then the St. Paul Seminary. Ordained in 1946, he taught at St. Thomas Military Academy, becoming headmaster in 1951. In 1968 the philosophy program at Nazareth Hall was closed and the St. John Vianney Seminary with its preliminary program was established on the College of St. Thomas campus. Father John Roach was its founding rector. When Roach assumed his duties as Archbishop, this was only the second time that a native son would preside in the area. Only John Ireland had done so before him. 1976 marked the bicentennial of the

The Cathedral of Saint Paul dome

"The things of the world and the things of faith derive from the same God"

Gaudium et Spes

United States and the National Council of Catholic Bishops sponsored a program, Liberty and Justice for All, and called all American Catholics to participate in the national observance. Local dioceses were to hold discussions and reflections in light of both Catholic tradition and the American political tradition concerning seven basic topics: the family, one's ethnic or racial group, the individual, the nation, the Church, and the world itself. Local meetings were to feed into regional meetings and in turn lead into the National Conference of Catholic Bishops in 1976. Monsignor Jerome Boxleitner was the archdiocesan coordinator for these local events.

Archbishop Roach saw revitalization and renewal in the Catholic Church in the archdiocese as a great source of optimism and hope. He regarded the Second Vatican Council as the most significant event in the 20th century. He was thrilled when that Council described the priest's role in the Church as a triple ministry: preaching the Gospel, shepherding the faithful, and celebrating divine worship. He lauded the Council fathers for advancing the reform of the liturgy, for furthering the Church's understanding of the fundamental equality of all baptized persons in vocation, dignity, and commitment, and for reversing previous attitudes toward other faiths through a commitment to further ecumenism.

When the Detroit diocese challenged American Catholics in 1976 through its "Call to Action" program, South Dakota farmers asked the bishops to address land tenure problems from a Catholic moral perspective. Roach participated in devising a regional Catholic bishops' statement on land issues entitled *Strangers and Guests - Toward Community in the Heartland.* Hearings were held in 12 heartland states in 1979. Forty-four dioceses were represented. A final draft of the document was signed by the bishops in Chicago, May 1, 1980.

Church of St. Olaf, Minneapolis

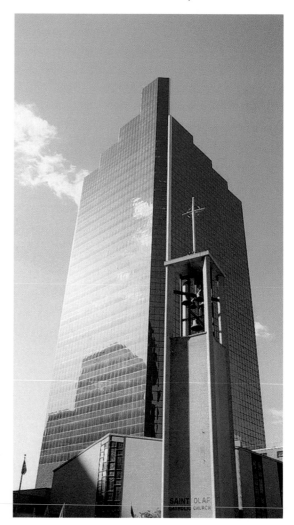

"Technical progress is of less value than advances toward greater justice, wider brotherhood, and a more humane social environment"

Gaudium et Spes

It was becoming obvious that for many the understanding of Church was changing as the whole people of God assumed more active roles in Church functions. The Church was the whole Church, not only the official Church in Rome, or the teaching Church, or the hierarchical Church. It was rather the living Church that works and prays, acts and meditates, remembers and searches. It was a sort of secret army recruited from everywhere, climbing unceasingly to perfect our nature. The Church was a silent witness that the gospel is always fruitful and that the Kingdom is already among us. Such a Church acknowledged a legitimate pluralism that allowed for diversity within its central doctrinal unity. It was necessary that the attendees of United States Bishops' Conference inserted their thinking into the process of dialogue about relevant issues. The Conference also profits from from the insights and experiences of others. This collegiality that united the bishops, including the Holy Father, expressed a special kind and degree of interrelationship. Archbishop Roach noted that bishops must be on guard that the United States Conference of Bishops not stifle legitimate local pluralism by becoming too specific and detailed in its formulations. A country as large and diverse as the United States is marked by regional differences and customs, attitudes, and even language. Could all of this diversity somehow be expressed in the local Church?

Old Church of St. Olaf ablaze, Minneapolis

Star Tribune Photo

"Bishops... along with their priests, are to preach the message of Christ in such a way that the light of the Gospel will shine on all activities of the faithful."

Gaudium et Spes

Vatican II had prompted much discussion on the role of the bishop in the contemporary Church. Roach saw bishops as official witnesses to the apostolic faith, having a unique share in and responsibility for preaching and teaching that faith throughout the world. Bishops taught through the celebration of the Eucharist and the other sacraments and public rites of the Church. They taught by using the electronic media. Sometimes bishops taught by positive judgment in conducting meetings with various groups within the diocese. There might also be need for negative judgment in pointing out unorthodox statements or theories of others. Bishops teach by their very presence as officials of the Church. Often when the Church is called upon to give prophetic witness to Gospel values, it cannot be ambivalent. Most often it is a single bishop who will speak out, because to delay response would make the reply irrelevant. There was always the question whether the U.S. Conference of Bishops could speak to contemporary times as a prophetic voice or did the necessity of consensus mute the Conference's voice?

Roach also saw his position as Archbishop as a ministry of service, to share with all the people of God the call of action to evangelize through the witness of word and deed. The bishop must call all the people of his diocese to action on behalf of the liberation and salvation of humanity. In these modern times bishops need to listen to new ministers whose sense of call to action is strong. The sacrifices these ministers make to remain in Church service are substantial. They need to be accepted and to know that the bishops of the Church do not have all the answers as to how best to address issues that arise. Bishops struggle with new ministers in bringing the Word to the contemporary world.

In attempting to form a community of believers, Roach was convinced that as Archbishop he should listen to women in the Church. The anger and pain of their discrimination were no longer hidden. Women expected justice within their Church. Roach felt that the bishops should lead in addressing the issues raised by women and not merely react to actions taken by women in striving for justice. Many more women were appointed to serve on archdiocesan boards and commissions. Archbishop Roach called for all American Bishops to listen to their Brown, Black, Red, brothers and sisters. He believed that his task as primary pastor was to form community. A bishop needed to remember what human nature is and not be afraid to make mistakes. Church leaders needed to respect mutuality and let others minister to them as they did to others. Nothing in community could be one-sided. All must respect life in its every aspect.

Roach also saw his role as archbishop as that of sanctifier. It was his duty to keep alive a vital sacramental ministry, yet safeguard a clear biblical spirituality that comes from the proclaimed Word. He must not neglect the need of each individual in his archdiocese - priest, deacon, and lay alike. He recognized the importance of a bishop's private space for personal piety, for individual counseling, and for the concern of the spiritual well-being of all of his people. He wanted to re-emphasize the role of religious as striving for holiness rather than as work, task- force personnel. Their lives of living faith should be seen as permeating the lives of all of the people of God with genuine evangelical values. Those values are Gospel values and are meant for the entire Church. New religious groups, such as the Brothers of Peace, were welcomed into the diocese.

Stained glass window, St. Anne's Church, Minneapolis

St. Joseph's Hospital, 1990's

"*The Church should have the freedom ... to pass moral judgments even in matters relating to politics, whenever the fundamental rights of humankind or the salvation of souls require it.*"

Gaudium et Spes

Archbishop Roach was an activist who believed strongly that a bishop must be involved in the political and economic issues of the day. The Church had to take action for justice and be in on the process of transforming the world as completely as possible into living the Gospel of Christ. As a leader, a bishop had to be willing to face the jeers, criticisms, and even prison bars in speaking out against the injustices of our times - the poverty, distress, and misery of all those in need.

Archbishop Roach was well aware of the need for auxiliary bishops to help with the growing demands of leadership in the archdiocese. In 1977 Bishop Paul Dudley and Bishop John Kinney became his auxiliaries. Roach consulted with various groups in the archdiocese before naming candidates for the episcopal ministry. Any priest, diocesan or religious, was eligible for recommendation. In 1980 Bishop J. Richard Ham replaced Bishop Dudley who was given a diocese of his own. In 1985 the archdiocese was divided into three vicariates with each auxiliary bishop overseeing the specific needs of the Church in that area. Bishop Carlson was in charge of St. Paul affairs, Bishop Bullock, Minneapolis, and Bishop Ham, the western and southern suburbs. These were times of rapidly shifting population in the archdiocese, a marked shortage of priests, and publicized sexual misconduct of some priests and Catholic teachers. Esteem for the priesthood was under fire in the media. In 1987 the archdiocese claimed 221 parishes and 600,000 Roman Catholics.

Ordination Mass of Bishop Paul Dudley and Bishop John Kinney

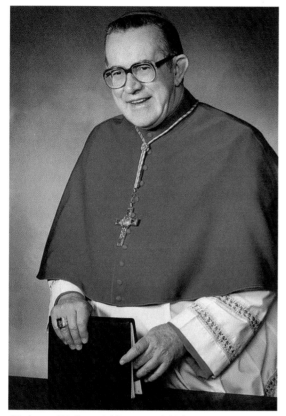

Bishop Richard Hamm, MM

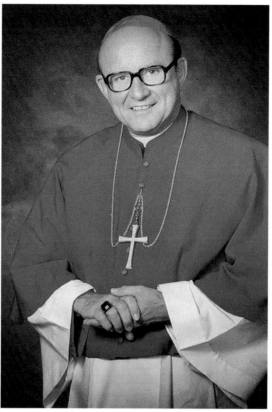

Bishop William Bullock

Bishop Robert Carlson

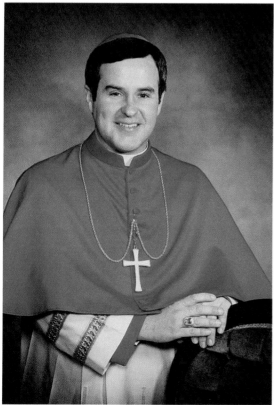

Bishop Joseph Charron, CPPS

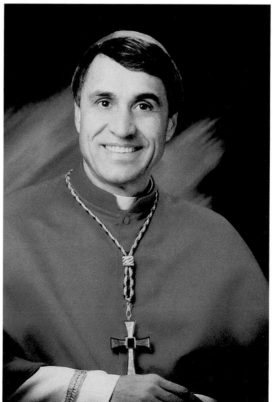

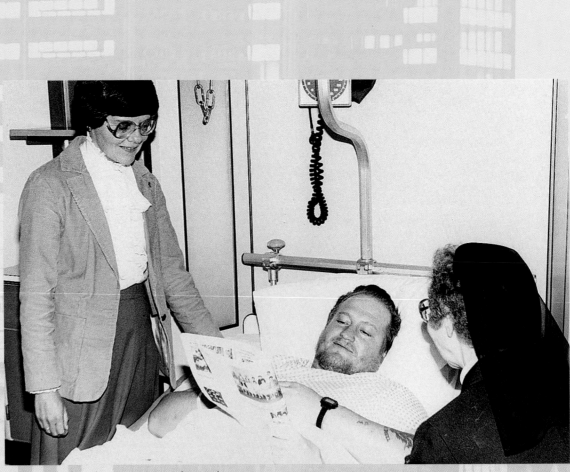

Hospital chaplains visiting the sick

The 1980s saw a further decline in the number of priests serving the archdiocese. Archbishop Roach, meanwhile, had assumed additional duties among the American hierarchy as vice president of the National Conference and then president from 1983 to 1985. The following year he was elected President of the Board of the National Catholic Life Conference. When his auxiliary bishops were given sees of their own, Roach's organizational vicariate plan for the archdiocese was thwarted. The shortage of priests and increasing demand for their services made staffing very difficult. Budgetary as well as staffing concerns of the Newman Center in Minneapolis fell more heavily on archdiocesan support during the 1970s and 1980s. Outside financial support for programs and maintenance had diminished, while personnel and programs had expanded. There was also a growing concern over staffing chaplains for area hospitals.

There were resident chaplains at the Catholic hospitals but local parishes took on the chaplain ministry at the other hospitals. The chaplain at Midway Hospital and the Cancer Home in St. Paul had to leave in order to assume a position in his religious community, creating another replacement need. The chancery tried to set up a program for parishes to rotate the responsibility to cover these facilities. The burden asked of local parishes was too great for them since they, too, had fewer priests to serve the parish needs. The question of utilizing the assistance of "dispensed priests" was widely discussed among the local clergy, but the policy adopted allowed them to serve as lectors, leaders of song, commentators, and extraordinary ministers of the Eucharist with permission of the archbishop. Such individuals could not serve in any official liturgical capacity or in a parish or institution where previously assigned.

"*Let them, as individuals and as group members, give a shining example to others.*"

Gaudium et Spes

When Archbishop Roach addressed his role of responsibility, along with priests and deacons of the diocese, in preaching the Word of God, he set forth guidelines for all with the special duty to carry out this function. All were thrilled when the ordination of the first permanent deacons took place after their long period of training. Archbishop Roach saw those in orders, priests and deacons, as his co-workers in preaching, a primary function tied to the Eucharist. Lay persons could preach in a church with the approval of the archbishop. Homilies were to draw out guiding principles from the Scriptures. Homilies were never to be omitted on Sundays and Holy days and were strongly encouraged for weekday liturgies, especially during Advent and Lent.

Ordination of first permanent deacons in Archdiocese

Ever an educator, Archbishop Roach was greatly concerned for implementing the Pope's call for spiritual renewal among all Church members. Prior to the 1976 Eucharistic Congress in Philadelphia, he authorized an Archdiocesan program of spiritual renewal to be conducted in the parishes prior to the Congress. This included catechesis, prayer, and apostolic action conducted during Lent with homilies, an adult lecture series, and special religious education features for the media. All were asked to share their food with the hungry of the world in a program called "Operation Rice Bowl." Roach promoted the 1st Annual Catholic Lay Celebration of Evangelization with its increased emphasis on models that included active participation and leadership of the laity. Working models in the Archdiocese included: Scripture Study Series, Outreach to Youth Program, Outreach to the Separated and Divorced Program, and Ministry to Alienated Catholics.

A call to spiritual renewal was addressed by the Faith Gathering experiences in the archdiocese which were very well received by the faithful. Archbishop Roach called the faithful to a deeper spirituality that would enhance their own lives and all others with whom they worked, prayed, played and dealt with in one way or another. Living the Gospel message was powerful enough to change the entire world for good. The first Faith Gathering in 1978 focused on the "School of Love" and dealt with prayer, friendship, liturgy and the Sacraments. Nationally known Catholic leaders, speakers, and writers were major presenters. People were very

Bishop Carslon at a gathering of Archdiocesan religious

Growth in personal holiness generated a greater concern for the plight of those in need. Under Roach's leadership the archdiocese expanded its contributions to the American Board of Catholic Missions. Donations grew from $43,000. in 1978 to $50,00 in 1984. In 1982 more than $716,000 was donated to the Society for the Propagation of the Faith. The Bureau of Catholic Indian Missions was among the recipients of this largesse. This agency in 1980 was proud to participate in the Beatification of the first American Indian, Kateri Tekakwitha, the Lily of the Mohawks. The National Council of Catholic Bishops supported this beatification and urged dioceses to send representatives from Indian communities within their areas to attend the beatification ceremonies. Deacon John Spears from Holy Rosary parish in Minneapolis was sent by the archdiocese for the festivities in Rome.

excited about the event and called for more. The 1979 meeting entitled "Hope for the Journey" addressed the United States' role in the arms race, Hispanics in the Church, Christian Feminism, Nuclear War Madness, and the Church's Role in the Social Order. The theme for 1984 was "Journeying Together Toward Peace."

Renew prayer group, Our Lady of Victory Church, Minneapolis

Following page: Worshippers at St. Peter Claver Church, Saint Paul

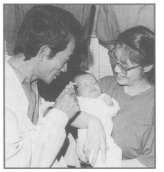

"One cannot underestimate the effect of emigration on those who, for whatever reason, are led to undertake a new way of life."

Gaudium et Spes

Although the post Vatican Church in America moved away from the immigrant Church of the early 1900s, contemporary immigration raised awareness of ethnic needs within the archdiocese. After the Vietnam War the archdiocese participated in the work of the American Refugee Committee organized to help the numbers of escaping refugees from Laos, Cambodia, and Vietnam. Local steering committees were under national offices in Washington, D.C. Marguerite Loftus served as archdiocesan program manager in helping these Asian refugees to resettle. She and her successors, Dick Flescher and Tom Kosel, have been aided by hundreds of laity in the parishes. Many of these helpers are still actively involved in assisting refugees to become acclimated to their new country. Tong Nguyen, an early refugee from Vietnam, acted as an interpreter for the archdiocesan refugee office. Through his efforts many Vietnamese Catholics settled in north Minneapolis, making St. Joseph's Church their parish church where their ethnic culture could flourish. The need of these immigrants to learn the English language was quickly addressed by volunteer programs sponsored by women religious and the archdiocesan bureau of Education. Centers that taught English as a second language sprang up. The more recent Bosnian refugees are currently finding mentors in Harry and Molly Thibault. Judy Mannella provides staff assistance to all seeking migration and refugee service. As secular society begins to address the needs of these new immigrants, collaboration among concerned groups will grow.

By the spring of 1980, there were about 2,500 Hmong in the Twin Cities area. By summer this number had increased to about 5,000.

Vietnamese family relocated in Minneapolis

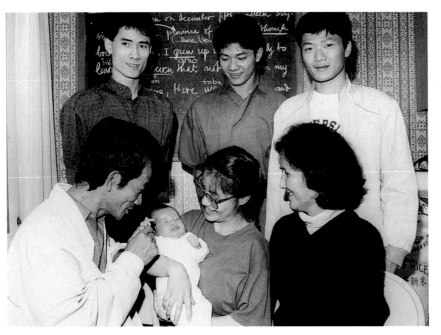

There were many Catholics among them. Catholic Charities directed them to seek help by joining a parish church. At the time only one Hmong catechist lived in the Twin Cities. Two diocesan priests had a Sunday Mass for the Hmong at which the catechist read the readings and preached in Hmong. But the Hmong community called for a priest of their own culture. In 1982 the archdiocese contracted with Father Daniel Taillez, O.M.I., at St. Mary's parish in lowertown St. Paul to work with the Hmong. Sister Teresa O'Brien, C.S.J., served them as pastoral minister in close contact with Father Taillez and Deacon Lo Vang Thai. This team organized ESL (English as a Second Language) classes and worked with Catholic Charities and the Human Services of Ramsey and Hennepin Counties to help the Hmong become acclimated to their new American home. Since there was no stable fund for food or clothing for these refugees, this team sought donations from many different charitable organizations.

The growing number of Hispanics in the archdiocese offered other opportunities. Since the early 1900s the West Side of St. Paul represented the highest concentration of Hispanics in Minnesota. The steady growth of Hispanic immigration after World War II found Hispanics scattered throughout the archdiocese. A 1978 poll showed that 90 percent of the Hispanics surveyed considered their Catholic faith and their culture inextricably linked and family was deemed their main educator. At that same time about 12 Protestant congregations had Hispanic followings in

Lee Pao Yang speaks about issues concerning Hmong Catholics

the Metropolitan area. After Vatican II most American Catholics relinquished many devotions, but the same was not true for Hispanics. While they might miss Mass on Sunday, Hispanics simply did not do so on festive occasions in which their devotions played a significant part. Over the years the Hispanics had reguested the use of their Spanish language and Latino customs. The archdiocese hired a Director of Hispanic Ministry in 1980 and invited the Saint Paul Seminary to have a part in the Hispanic Ministry in the Archdiocese. Under Roach's leadership, the American Council of Catholic Bishops formulated a Pastoral Statement on Hispanic Ministry. They noted that Hispanic Catholics wanted to offer their historical, cultural, and religious gifts to the Church which they saw as their home and their heritage. Historically, no other European culture had been in the country longer than the Hispanic. The bishops called for religious and lay leaders workers at harvest time to include cultural aspects of Hispanics in the liturgy, for more Hispanic permanent deacons, for a greater use of the Spanish language in Catechesis, for setting up special youth programs for them, and for

Workers at harvest time

Jose Gomez leads church singing

training Hispanics for Church ministries, especially as preachers. In the archdiocese, although Hispanics had moved into all sections of the metropolis, Our Lady of Guadalupe Church on St. Paul's West Side became the focus of implementing the bishops' directive.

Archbishop Roach did much to further better relations between Catholics and Jews, not only in the archdiocese but throughout America. In St. Paul, Roach worked with Jewish and Protestant leaders through the Joint Religious Legislative Coalition in getting public assistance for the poor through food stamps, child support enforcement, hospitalization for the needy.

124

and housing, energy, and land use concerns. In 1983 The Jewish Community Relations Council and the Anti Defamation League of Minnesota and the Dakotas presented Roach with the Samuel Scheiner Award in recognition for his tireless dedication and humanitarian concern in advancing human rights and interreligious and interracial harmony.

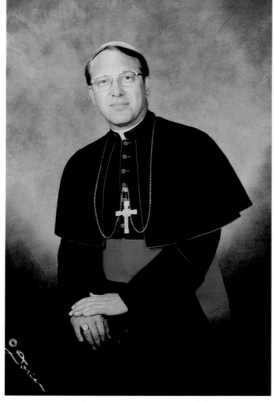

Bishop Lawrence Welsh

law in 1978 that mandated public service to handicapped children within non-public schools across the state. At the same time a Director of Special Education for the archdiocese was appointed and lay leaders called for a minister to the handicapped as well. Nathalie Welch was an active promoter for the archdiocese to address the

He was also honored for his work in arousing the world's conscience to the grave moral implications of nuclear war through the efforts of the National Council of Catholic Bishops. In August, 1987, Archbishop Roach represented the NCCB at a meeting in Rome to establish a commission for the purpose of drawing up an official Catholic statement on the Holocaust. Roach called for educators to strive to show the unity of biblical revelation (Old Testament and New) in God's plan of salvation. Catholics owned the Old Testament as much as the Jews. Yet, the Church and all Christians must read the Old Testament in the light of the event of the death-resurrection of Christ. Christian and Jewish identity should nevertheless be carefully distinguished in their respective reading of the Bible.

The Catholic Education Center of the archdiocese, through lobbying Minnesota legislators, dispelled the myth that Catholic schools simply rejected the admission of handicapped youngsters in the parochial system. That office influenced the passage of the Minnesota

problems of the handicapped in liturgies, conferences, and building accessibility.

Addressing a ministry to gays and lesbians in the local Church became an important issue when the question of hiring homosexual teachers in parochial schools arose. Archdiocesan voices, clergy and lay, called for church leaders of all denominations to help society find ways to guarantee homosexuals every civil and human right without their conduct becoming a violation of the rights of others. By condemning the acts of homosexuality and not the persons, the Catholic Church was seen as not accepting the sexual orientation of gays and lesbians. Members of the homosexual community conducted protest demonstrations against what they called this unjust Church stance. The growing number of AIDS victims in the region prompted further pressure from concerned priests, religious, and laity who were already ministering to these needy victims and their families. These urged Archbishop Roach to establish an AIDS Ministry in the archdiocese.

Chuck Ceronsky, who served as chair of the task force for the diocese, and Father Leo Tibesar turned their pastoral care training to the cause. Nine priests immediately volunteered to be ready to assist with this ministry. St. Mary's Hospital provided office space for the AIDS Ministry and Sister Joanne Lucid, BVM was chosen to staff the effort. The Center for Religious Education at the College of St. Thomas was asked to assist the Pastoral Health Care Commission in providing training programs for all pastoral ministers in the archdiocese, since it was supposed that every minister would encounter individuals and families affected by AIDS. Roach became convinced that the Church needed to link itself with the compassionate example and teaching of Jesus in following a truly Christian course of action. He called for all to become better educated on the nature of AIDS so that we could best deal with the inevitable fact of AIDS in parishes, schools and families. As an active participant in the National Council of Catholic Bishops, Roach was instrumental in that conference's statement, The Many Faces of AIDS: A Gospel Response." This was a statement of compassion and a plea for prevention. As such, it had teaching dimensions for the Church.

The archdiocese strengthened its stance on the right to life after the *Roe vs. Wade* decision of the Supreme Court in 1973. American bishops collectively condemned the decision as fraught with national shame. The MCCL (Minnesota Citizens concerned for Life) strengthened its ranks and continued to educate the entire area of the evils of abortion. Archbishop Roach championed strong educational efforts to convince people of the need for constitutional protection of unborn human life. He worked hard for

the NCCB to encourage the bishops to call for a Right to Life Amendment to the Constitution. He lobbied senators and representatives in Washington to support legislation authorizing such an amendment. The U.S. Catholic Conference and the NCCB supported the Hatch Amendment which claimed that the unborn child is a person under the law in terms of the Constitution from conception on. In 1983 the Hatch Amendment was defeated in Congress. An area Catholic philosopher, specializing in medical ethics, argued that there were solid reasons for not including early human embryos under the full weight and protection of the Church law against abortions. The debate over when life began kept the abortion question alive.

Roach pursued a practical approach to the abortion issue. Wanting to help young women with unwanted pregnancies he formed an ad hoc Committee on the Adoption Option. This committee prepared a brochure and found support and cooperation with the Seton Program, Catholic Charities, the Children's Home Society of Minnesota, and the Lutheran Social Services of Minnesota. This became a non-profit corporation with Patricia Maxeiner as president.

The right to life issue also began to focus on the needs of the terminally ill, especially with the publicity given to those who promote euthanasia. Within the archdiocese the Sisters of the Hawthorne Dominicans had for years offered a free terminal cancer home which gave historical balance to the growing work of hospice providers. The hospice philosophy stressed the value of life, restoring the fundamental family and religious ideals that have nourished American civilization. In the early 1990s there were 13 hospice programs in the

Euthanasia demonstration

Twin Cities - Catholic, Protestant, Jewish, and a few without religious affiliation. A study of these showed about 150 local physicians and 100 caregivers participating in hospice care. Area Catholic hospitals, dedicated pastors and laypersons were in the forefront of this new social movement in America. Dr. Elizabeth Kubler Ross' book, *On Death and Dying,* had electrified the health care system of the United States.

Catholic leaders, clerical and lay, wanted the archdiocese to show greater concern for other family problems, especially the divorced, separated, widowed and those in second marriages. A Catholic Marriage Course for persons entering a second marriage was offered at the University of St.

Thomas and proved to be highly successful. The Marriage Encounter Program was established in the archdiocese. In weekend retreat-like meetings, couples focused on increased communication, dealing with true feelings. Spearheaded by staunch lay leaders like Tom and Norma Kenny, this program enriched the lives of married couples of all ages and influenced active participation in parish activities. The issues of violence in the family, including child abuse, incest, and battering were of great concern to secular and religious leaders alike. In 1980 Roach participated in Governor Al Quie's conference entitled, "Battered Women, the Religious Response." In 1986 Archbishop Roach campaigned against the Congressional bill to cut AFDC by 30 percent. He wrote to congressmen as president of NCCB, spoke before the Minnesota Senate Finance Committee against these cuts, and got Minnesota Senator Durenberger to support the Bishops' position against the bill.

Church of St. Odilia, Shoreview

"Forms of social or cultural discrimination on the grounds of sex, race, color, social conditions, language or religion, must be curbed and eradicated as incompatible with God's design."

Gaudium et Spes

Although women religious throughout the country called for public Church support in the matter of equality for women in American society, the National Council of Catholic Bishops decided to maintain a neutral position on the Equal Rights Amendment. The failure of Congress to pass the ERA did not enhance the position of women within the American Church. In the eyes of the hierarchy the ordination of women to the priesthood became a moot question and even the ordination of women as deacons was rejected. Despite that fact, wives of deacons were required to go through the formal training with their spouses. Roach did not want action prompting the debate about the ordination of women deacons to come from the Permanent Diaconate of the Archdiocese. There simply would be no dialogue on this issue. The Archdiocesan Commission on Women and the Sisters' Council tried to keep the issue alive, but they were advised to drop the issue. Nevertheless, Roach did establish an Archdiocesan Commission on Women in 1979, and began appointing women to positions of leadership in his administration.

The increased number of the aged in contemporary society made many leaders in the diocese aware of the growing needs of the elderly. Sister Mary Madonna Ashton, C.S.J., then the Commissioner of Public Health in Minnesota, approached the Archbishop with the petition to form an ad hoc committee for the diocese that would address the concerns of the elderly. Roach wanted to leave this concern to other agencies. But when federal cutbacks in

energy allocations to the state were made, he asked that parishes form a communication network to check on the elderly and the poor during the winter months. He asked his priests to implement this appeal. He charged Catholic Charities to assist pastors in establishing a program to help the elderly. He helped further the work of the Westminister Corporation, an agency known as Common Bond, to obtain funds to build and manage housing for the poor, the elderly, and the disabled. Catholic Eldercare was established in northeast Minneapolis with archdiocesan support.

Over the years, Catholic Charities grew into the largest non-governmental social-service agency in the metropolitan area. With about 75 programs at 30 different sites in the 1990s, Catholic Charities serves the community's poor, including the homeless, immigrants, elderly, troubled youth, AIDS patients, and others in need. Based on a philosophy of compassion for the poor, Catholic Charities, largely through the intrepid leadership of Monsignor J. Jerome Boxleitner, who directed the agency for over 35 years, strove to put faces on those in need and uphold their dignity as persons. The helping hands of those working with Catholic Charities often came face to face with justice issues that needed to be addressed at governmental levels.

"*Among nations there is a growing movement to set up a worldwide community.*"

Gaudium et Spes

The years of Archbishop Roach's leadership in the archdiocese were marked by an attempt of the local Church to address justice issues, not only locally but globally. Many among the faithful assumed the role of leadership and forged ahead in addressing the needs of the marginalized of society. Sister Mary Giovanni, SSND worked tirelessly, pleading for funds from the state, the archdiocese, and area foundations to support her projects with the Mexican-Americans in Guadalupe parish. The work of her religious community with the poor people of Guatemala brought focus to the flagrant violation of human rights in that country encouraged by the economic policy of the United States toward Guatemala. Protecting human rights in foreign lands became a major justice issue of the National Council of Catholic Bishops.

Sister Giovanni, SSND, pleads for a new school

> *"It is to the laity... to cultivate a properly informed conscience and to impress the divine law on the affairs of the earthly city."*
>
> *Gaudium et Spes*

Minneapolis skyline

Americans were horrified when the media reported the killings of the Maryknoll Sisters and lay volunteer in El Salvador in 1980. Killings of religious and lay missionaries continued, suggesting a real persecution of the Church in that region. In other countries of Central America there was evidence of disregard for the sanctity of life. Archbishop Roach called for strong prayers of the faithful in the archdiocese that social justice and protection of human rights for the people of the entire region be realized. He used his clout as president of the NCCB to remind Congress not to become callous in the deaths of religious, priests, and catechists that were taking place in Central America. Prodded by lay leaders in the diocese, Roach authorized the establishment of the Minnesota Center for Medical and

Legal Aspects of Torture. The center provided medical, psychiatric, and legal services for victims of torture and similar human rights violations. Many religious felt drawn to this ministry and withdrew from previously held ministries, which were involved with issues not nearly as life-threatening. This was the first such institution in the United States. When nuns raised concern over archdiocesan investments in South Africa, Roach was instrumental in getting the U.S. Catholic Conference to adopt a policy statement in 1986 on South Africa, Divestment, and Disinvestment. This was directly linked to the fact that the government of South Africa failed to undertake significant steps toward dismantling apartheid and negotiating with Black leaders. He called for the United States government to use its considerable power to effect a political and social solution to the problem rather than provide weaponry to continue a useless war. The Archdiocesan Urban Affairs Commission, Chaired by Mary Lou Klas, endorsed the Nuclear Freeze Campaign, Roach endorsed the campaign as a call for the U.S. and the Soviet Union to stop the nuclear arms race and adopt a mutual freeze on the testing, production, and development of nuclear weapons. Roach got 50,000 signatures in Minnesota in support of the Albert Einstein Peace Prize Foundation resolution which went both to the U.S. Government and also to the U.S.S.R. urging negotiations for nuclear arms reduction.

"*God destined the earth and all it contains...*
for all peoples so that all created things
would be shared fairly..."

Gaudium et Spes

When the problems of farmers escalated in the 1980s, the area bishops met at St. John's in Collegeville to establish a task force of members from the American Lutheran Church, the Lutheran Church of America, and the Minnesota Catholic Conference. The task force drafted a statement on the critical farm issue and forwarded it to the two senators from Minnesota. They noted that the economic crisis for farmers was the result of high concentrations of economic power in the United States. This evolved into a spiritual and moral crisis for farmers who felt government policies made them unworthy, stripped them of their dignity, and blamed them as victims of their own predicament. The bishops called for just prices for the farmers, protection of their land and aid to regenerate their farms. They wanted government aid to ensure that more people would have the

opportunity to participate in farming. In 1985 it became clear that the farmers needed help in their dealings with the Farmer's Home Administration. The Minnesota Legal Services Coalition distributed the Farmers' Guide to the Farmer's Home Administration which described approaches farmers could take in dealing with the Administration and also explained the farmer's legal rights. Archbishop Roach worked with members of the Mid-Minnesota Legal Assistance, Inc. to write bills that were to be directed to the Supreme Court, guaranteeing expanded legal services for farmers. Roach also garnered help from the Hamline University School of Law in this venture. In 1986 Roach was elected President of the Board of the National Catholic Rural Life Conference which served as a national office for all diocesan rural life directors and issued position

Contemporary farm family doing chores

131

Father Thomas Wrzos offers consolation to a prisoner

statements on national legislation regarding food and agriculture, seeking the implementation of a just food system for the United States. Many people wondered if the Church should get involved in issues which they regarded as public policy. Roach's response was that the Church must speak to those issues in order to translate traditional teaching into relevant public terms for contemporary society. The Second Vatican Council mandated that the Church stand as a sign and safeguard of the dignity of the person in the political order. Roach maintained that human dignity, human rights, and human life were at stake. As early as 1975 priests and laity of the archdiocese petitioned Roach to establish an archdiocesan office for global justice. A World Justice and Peace Commission was authorized which collaborated with the Urban Affairs Commission, known for its attacks on American capitalism as exploitative and unjust.

The "pedophilia problem" among the clergy caused troubling notoriety for the American Church in the late 1980s. Pressures were put on the archdiocese to address its in-house sexual abuse problems. Archbishop Roach and Catholic clergy in general received bad press month after month feeding into prevalent anti-clerical and anti-Catholic attitudes. Roach adopted a policy that covered the pastoral response to sexual misbehavior by ministry personnel and

mandated all archdiocesan personnel to be given sexual awareness training.

The Newman Center at the University of Minnesota was permitted to sponsor Dignity, a local chapter of a nationwide association of gay Catholics. When the Holy See described homosexuality as an intrinsic disorder, yet allowing homosexuals to participate in Mass if they remained celibate, Archbishop Roach asked members of Dignity to sign a statement in support of the Church's teaching. Dignity members refused and a difficult public seperation followed. The personal failure in judgment of the archbishop in his DWI arrest in February 1985 provided additional grist for the anti-Church press of both local and national newspapers. Roach grew as a compassionate pastor through this incident.

He became a strong leader in promoting Reverend John Forliti's Catholic Sex Education Program. He encouraged the Catholic Education Center to issue a strong statement on pre-marital sex and to appoint someone from the Catholic Education Center to be responsible for training catechists in this area. Roach called on parents who had the primary role in guiding and supporting their youngsters. In 1990 he published a pamphlet entitled *Teen Sexuality, A Guide for Parents and Teenagers*. In addition the archdiocese developed a program aimed at expanding communication on sexuality between parents and children, parish-based support groups for parents, and a variety of initiatives to reinforce Catholic teaching in sexual morality for adolescents and enhance their ability to say "no" to sexual activity before marriage. The increased adolescent pregnancies, abortion problems, and the spread of AIDS were of great concern to all Church leaders.

> # "*The unity of Christians is today awaited and longed for by many...*"
>
> *Gaudium et Spes*

Archbishop Roach consistently worked for ecumenism both at the local and national levels. It had become evident to priests serving in the military during the Vietnam War years that they needed to minister to men of different religious persuasions. When asked for guidance from their bishop in these matters, Archbishop Roach, looking to the pastoral intent of the bishops of Vatican II, said that it was preferable that no general norms, much less specific rites, be introduced which would interfere with the legitimate diversity that existed. The decision for ministry had to rest with the chaplain who should always act with respect for the individual in need.

In 1982, after 12 years of work by a joint commission established by Pope John Paul II and the Archbishop of Canterbury, the Anglican-Roman Catholic Report on Authority in the Church was published. Although not yet in full communion, it seemed that substantial agreement on some divisive issues was possible. It opened the way for new steps to be taken to deepen reconciliation and make a forward thrust in quest of full communion. Roach and the American Council of Bishops endeavored to further these steps at their diocesan levels. They sought the development of a standard pattern for pastoral ministry to ecumenical marriages between Anglicans and Roman Catholics, promoting further meetings on a regional basis between the bishops of the two Churches, and maintaining dialogue between the two Churches on significant issues facing America, such as: Central America, Nuclear Armaments, the Hatch Amendment, and

capital punishment. The Supreme Court now allowed states to opt for capital punishment, reversing a previous court decision.

Over the years, largely through the Joint Religious Legislative Coalition, collaboration had grown among the leaders of various Churches in the metropolitan area. By 1990, this growing trust enabled the local Church leaders to sign a covenant committing their faith communities to a common witness and mission. Archbishop John Roach, Bishop Lowell Erdahl of the Evangelical Lutheran Church in America (St. Paul Area Synod) and Bishop Olson of the ELCA (Minneapolis Area Synod) signed the covenant in a ceremony in the St. Paul Cathedral. In this joint effort in the quest for peace and justice, these leaders thanked God for the unity He gave them to celebrate in joint services, and they prayed for the day when they could celebrate the Eucharist as one community. This agreement provided those who live in a Catholic-Lutheran covenant in their families with special support and paved the way for studying jointly the public conversations of the national Catholic-Lutheran dialogues and for acting jointly on recommendations of the respective Churches in response.

During these years Roach, showed a strong commitment to ecumenism. He had considerable communication with Apostolic Delegate Jean Jadot, D. D., Ph.D., whom Pope John Paul II would later name to head the Secretariat for Non-Christians. Roach tolerated no adverse criticism of Jadot's suggestions toward ecumenism for the American

Church by the local arch-conservative Catholic press. Jadot came to the archdiocese and had dialogues with the Priests' Senate, faculties of the St. Paul Seminary and the St. John Vianney Preparatory Seminary, directors of diocesan departments, the Pastoral Council, Sisters' Council, and leaders of the Deaneries. Jadot officiated at the celebration of Mass at the College of St. Thomas on the patronal feast of the college.

"*The laity are called to participate actively in the whole life of the Church.*"

Gaudium et Spes

Archbishop Roach's vision for the local Church had been to address the needs of the people of God under his jurisdiction to strengthen their parish worship, to promote every Christian's ministerial responsibility for the Church, to champion justice for all by following the thrust of the Detroit Call to Action Conference, to help strengthen family life through marriage and family commissions, to implement an adult Christian formation program for preparing adults for ministry at the parish, school, deanery, and archdiocesan levels, and to foster personal and spiritual growth of young Catholics from birth through high school through commitment to formal Catholic education at all levels. He strove to collaborate with clergy, religious, and laity to achieve his goals for the archdiocese. His mode of delegation was based on trust. He assigned tasks and trusted that they would get done. He

Archbishop Harry J. Flynn in Rome

was an artful consulter, listening to various perspectives and then pulling them together for realistic action. His common sense and good humor peppered his forceful talks about issues that required the articulation of the Church's position on them. On his 70th birthday Archbishop Roach shared some of his vision of what lay ahead for the archdiocese. There would always be new planning cycles as new issues and new needs arose in society. He predicted no dramatic change in the decreasing number of priestly vocations. Yet, he believed that strong prayer and energy applied to the vocation question would encourage those hesitating to take first steps toward the priesthood. He was convinced that the Church would continue to develop and refine lay ministry, both professional and volunteer, and that the laity would be an ongoing source of strength for the Church as abortion, euthanasia, and

134

Archbishop Harry J. Flynn

other life issues continued to plague society. The struggle ahead would be a mighty one to maintain a genuine sanctity of life in America. Although no one knew exactly what lay ahead for the American Church, Roach called all to the conviction that the Lord would continue to strengthen His ministers. He called all to hope in the future because God had made promises to His people, promises which He never takes lightly.

In October, 1993 Archbishop Roach requested a coadjutor to assist him in leading the Archdiocese. His fears of losing his current auxiliaries, Bishop Robert Carlson and Bishop Joseph Charron became realities when Bishop Charron was named Bishop of Des Moines and Bishop Carlson was named coadjutor Bishop of Sioux Falls. On February 22, 1994 Archbishop Harry J. Flynn was appointed Coadjutor Archbishop of the Archdiocese of St. Paul and Minneapolis, with right of succession. This New York native and former Bishop of Lafayette, Louisiana, shared fully in the decision-making and

responsibility of the archdiocese until Roach formally retired. While working with Flynn on the Administrative Board of the National Conference of Catholic Bishops, Roach had been impressed by Flynn's wisdom, his genuine sense of the sacred character of other people, his sense of social justice, and his enormous love of the Church. Archbishop Flynn began his ministry in the archdiocese on April 27, 1994.

HARRY JOSEPH FLYNN was born May 2, 1933 in Schenectady, New York of Irish lineage. After attending parochial schools through high school and Sienna College in Loudonville, he graduated from Mt. St. Mary Seminary in Emmitsburg, Maryland, and was ordained in 1960. He ministered as parish priest and high school teacher for five years in Troy, New York, and became Dean of Men at Mount St. Mary Seminary in 1965. From 1970 until 1981 he served as Rector of the Mount. In 1986, he became Coadjutor Bishop of Lafayette, Louisiana, and assumed duties as Lafayette's fourth bishop in 1989. Named Coadjutor Archbishop of St. Paul and Minneapolis in 1994, he assumed the responsibilities as archbishop in 1995.

Archbishop Roach introduces coadjutor Archbishop Flynn at a news conference

> ## "*The Church is universal in that it is not committed to any one culture or to any political, economic or social system.*"
>
> *Gaudium et Spes*

At Archbishop Flynn's inaugural Mass in 1994, worshippers were reminded of the diversity of the archdiocese by the several languages used in the Mass celebration. Archbishop Flynn was introduced to his 12 county archdiocese with its 222 parishes, dozens of schools, and more than 40 archdiocesan agencies serving a variety of ministries. The region was larger, and far more multi-ethnic than areas where he had previously ministered. He brought to the archdiocese a wealth of pastoral experience. While Coadjutor Bishop of Lafayette, he had served as a delegate to the Pope's Synod of Bishops. He sat on the NCCB Domestic Policy Committee, the Nominating Committee for conference officers, and the Ad Hoc Committee on Sexual Abuse formed to help bishops deal with clergy sexual abuse. This friendly and outgoing archbishop, who demonstrated a fantastic ability to remember names, impressed his new flock as a pastoral leader who liked people, liked to be with them, and who liked to hear stories as well as tell them himself. His love of

Archbishop Flynn

the church and belief that everything is Christ-centered is reflected in the motto on his coat of arms, "Come Lord Jesus," which also heads his weekly column in the official organ of the archdiocese. He changed the name of that paper to *The Catholic Spirit* , emphasizing the on-going presence of Christ in the work of His contemporary Church. He quickly was perceived as a strong man of prayer with a penchant to speak his mind, never leaving others in doubt where he stood on an issue. In facing hard decisions and difficult times in leadership, he relies on his good sense of humor. His work with youth and the black community in Lafayette had endeared him to many, adding to an already voluminous personal correspondence. Over the years he has been a staunch supporter of the Pro-Life Movement. As Bishop of Lafayette, he spoke out against capital punishment in an area of the country where those views are very unpopular. He felt compelled to help educate people in the teachings of the Church.

*Cathedral of
Saint Paul
from the High Bridge*

"*The Church believes that the center and the purpose
of the whole of human history is to be found
in its Lord and Master.*"

Gaudium et Spes

The new archbishop was faced with a host of concerns needing pastoral attention. Social service issues were fraught with problems of domestic violence, racial discrimination, fair wages, full employment, and the need for welfare and health care reform. Affordable and permanent housing for children and other children's issues had to be top priorities but there was the reality of diminishing resources. Aware of a host of willing and capable lay ministers, Flynn had to address two major problems: adequate financial compensation and how to finance on-going education for those involved in Church ministry. The archbishop feels obliged to recognize and use the rich talent and treasure that lie in the well-educated laity, some more highly educated than the priests, yet uphold the special role of the clergy in all diocesan organizations. The tremendous diversity of the region encouraged areas of ministry relating to the empowerment of all people, women as well as men, and

*Archbishop Flynn
visits with
retired sisters*

137

people of all different educational backgrounds and races. Flynn is also concerned about finding economical ways to train catechists. He recognizes the need for providing a solid training for catechists in theology. He knows that he must become more familiar and informed about the issues facing rural communities of the Midwest. He believes that the people expect him to speak out on farm issues when occasions warrant it. Above all, Archbishop Flynn recognizes that Catholics on the banks of the Mississippi River in Minnesota have taken leadership roles in three prime areas addressed by Vatican II: the liturgy, social justice, and lay ministry. The music of Marty Haugen, Michael Joncas, and David Haas is being used in dioceses across the nation. The influence of the late Monsignor John A. Ryan in addressing social justice issues is evident. There are more professional lay ministers in the Archdiocese of St. Paul and Minneapolis than in any other metropolitan see in the United States. Archbishop Flynn believes it is important to assess the needs throughout the archdiocese and to look at the parishes and determine whether or not the personnel are being adequately used and whether their gifts are being used properly. He maintains that one of the beauties that resulted from the Second Vatican Council is the special call of the laity to assume more active roles in the functions of the Church. So many of the laity are bringing forth their gifts for Church ministry. It is important that these gifts be celebrated.

Early 1999, Archbishop Flynn faced the loss of his auxiliary bishop, the much beloved Bishop Lawrence Welsh, who died after a long illness. Ordained Bishop of Spokane, Washington in 1978, Welsh was named Auxiliary Bishop of the Archdiocese in 1991. In 1996, he was named vicar for Hispanic affairs and did much to address the needs of the Hispanics in the archdiocese. He had a gift of uplifting the poor as he ministered to them, often showing up at various Catholic Charities outlets in the Twin Cities, feeding the poor and talking with them. In these situations he wanted to be seen as just another member of the people of God, and never identified himself as a bishop. His loss was felt deeply in the ranks of both clergy and laity.

In addressing the problem of the shortage of priests in the archdiocese, Archbishop Flynn believes that in the future it may be necessary for some parishes to merge. Yet, no parish should be dissolved. Good planning, careful collaboration, and good will on everyone's part will be essential. He sees the role of deacons expanding, as more men take this step to ordination. He sees little likelihood that the laicized clergy would very soon be called on to alleviate some of our overextended clergy. If this comes, he thinks that it will take a long time to materialize and then roles must be clearly defined. In addressing his perception of the role of religious in Church ministry, Archbishop Flynn is of a mind that new recruits to the various groups of religious will be few if the religious groups do not articulate well their corporate witness. He recognizes that his view may be open for debate. There can be no question of the archbishop's commitment to foster vocations. He invites potential candidates for the seminary and for religious communities to special dinners held in his residence. Through these programs called "Operation Andrew" and "Operation Miriam" the archbishop encourages discussion and demonstrates his concern and support for these budding vocations.

> **"*I*n the light of the Second Vatican Council it is to be hoped that public opinion in the Church would present the opportunity... for establishing dialogue."**
>
> *Gaudium et Spes*

Archbishop Flynn believes strongly that women must be given the opportunity for responsibility in Church ministry, but not as ordained priests since that parameter has been set by Rome's teaching, and dialogue on that subject accomplishes nothing. We must not give the impression, he says, that through dialogue we will change this. He believes that if women are to own the Church more completely, they have to have some voice in determining the future of the Church. Right now in time women can do this through accepting responsible positions. How this plays out is really unknown, but at the Synod of 1990 the women present there made longer interventions than did the men. This had an effect on the thinking of many of the assembled bishops.

Such dissent within the Church will continue and the archdiocese will have its share of dissenters. While Archbishop Flynn feels that there is room for the expression of divergent opinions on controversial issues in the Church, nevertheless, he cautions all to be very sensitive to the faith of those who are struggling with important decisions in their lives. Fragile consciences ought not be marred by individuals bent on bringing changes that they champion. In the area of Catholic education, Archbishop

Flynn calls all levels of Catholic Education to be more racially inclusive. He thinks that the archdiocesan thrust must be more pro-active in inviting minorities - African-Americans, American Indians, Vietnamese, Mexican-Americans, and others- into our Catholic schools, and even try to provide scholarships where needed. Our Catholic schools must provide a solid grounding in the tenets of the Catholic Church and prepare our youth to assume responsible positions for living their faith whatever career they choose.

Archbishop Harry Flynn speaks with great pride of the many accomplishments of Catholic Charities in the archdiocese. The current Board of Catholic Charities, under the chairmanship of Karen Rauenhorst, has developed a re-organizational plan for that agency. Even though Flynn has been in the archdiocese a short time, he believes that Catholic Charities is one of the most effective agencies in the archdiocese. He anticipates great things from Catholic Charities in the future.

Pope John Paul II meets with archdiocesan youth in Denver, 1992

> ## *"There is no human law so powerful to safeguard the personal dignity and freedom of all as the Gospel entrusted to the Church."*
>
> *Gaudium et Spes*

Flynn wants to continue addressing justice issues through the Minnesota Conference, his own office, and the Archdiocesan Office for Social Justice. Social justice must be everyone's concern, yet these particular groups have special leadership roles to alert the rest of the people and call them to actions in order to promote change in the greater society. Many issues facing our society need a grounding in basic Christian principles: questions about *Humanae Vitae,* abortion, euthanasia, genetic experimentation, all the health issues, living will, just war issues. With an eye to the future, Archbishop Flynn reminds the faithful of the line from Dante: "In Thy will is our peace, O God." He sees the need to connect people to the belief that there is only peace and happiness in finding out the will of God and then embracing it. As Church leader, he must strive to explain that finding that will is not always easy. An area of grave concern for him is that the American Church has not really done a good job of proclaiming the traditional teaching of the Church on the respect for the dignity of each person. All believers need to stress that every person is made in the image and likeness of God and that God knows each person's name at every moment. Flynn lauds the efforts of Archbishop Roach and his commitment to make sure that on every level of education in our seminaries, in our high schools, in our grade schools there will be an effort to teach and to incorporate into the curriculum all the social teachings of the Church, laid down in the Catholic social encyclicals, the best kept secret of the nation.

Bishop Welsh leads procession at St. Thomas Becket groundbreaking

State Capitol Building, Saint Paul

As Archbishop Harry Flynn faces the many challenges of leading the people of God in the Saint. Paul and Minneapolis Archdiocese into the Church of the 21st century, he hopes to be able to address the issues of ecumenism that would draw Catholics and Protestants closer in living out the Gospel message. He lauds the outstanding work of the Archdiocesan Ecumenical Commission and hopes to further that work through more active participation. He is realistic about time constraints put on one archbishop in so large a local Church.

FATHER FREDERIC CAMPBELL was ordained auxiliary bishop for the Archdiocese on May 14, 1999 to assist Archbishop Flynn with the task of shepherding the people of the Archdiocese.

As he faces the coming millennium, Archbishop Harry Flynn takes pride in all that his predecessors have accomplished for the Church in this area. He hopes to contribute to that legacy by implementing a pastoral approach in his leadership in the archdiocese. The thrust of Vatican II must go on to keep the Church relevant to changing times and new challenges. He believes that a bishop's pastoral approach will enable

people to know their bishop as a pastor who is concerned about them as persons. They may not always agree with him, but they will surely know that he has great concern for each individual and that they, as the People of God, contribute to the fulfillment of Christ's mandate for the Church, to live His Gospel message until the end of time.

Bishop Campbell

*The people of God believes that
it is led by the Spirit of the Lord
who fills the whole world."*

Gaudium et Spes

Acknowledgments

Special thanks to the following individuals who contributed their time and talent to make this project a reality.

Archbishop Harry Flynn

Father Kevin McDonoungh

Sister John Christine Wolkerstorfer

Members of the 150th Anniversary Planning Committee

Timothy Anderson

Patrick Anzelc and the Archives Office

Photos Contributed By:

Doug Ohman, Pioneer Photography

Catholic Spirit Newspaper

Archives Office, Archdiocese of Saint Paul and Minneapolis

Minnesota Historical Society

Frantisek Zvardon